RISKY
LIVING

JAMIE
BUCKINGHAM

RISKY LIVING

Keys to Inner Healing

LOGOS INTERNATIONAL
Plainfield, New Jersey

RISKY LIVING: Keys to Inner Healing
Copyright © 1976 by Logos International
All Rights Reserved
Printed in the United States of America
Published by Logos International, Plainfield, N.J. 07061
International Standard Book Numbers: 0-88270-175-4 (hardcover)
0-88270-177-0 (softcover)
Library of Congress Catalog Card Number: 76-12033

CONTENTS

FOREWORD

In a recent issue of *Reader's Digest* I ran across an article by the renowned architect, Peter Blake, who is also editor-in-chief of an international publication called *Architecture Plus*. In the opening paragraph of his article, Blake said:

> There exists a great temptation, in the life of an artist or scientist or modern architect like myself, to commit oneself to a dogma in one's youth and then to build one's entire work on that foundation. Unhappily for me and for some of my friends, the premises upon which we have almost literally built our world are crumbling.

As I read I realized Blake was not talking just about architecture and architects. He was talking about theology, about life. He was talking about me, about my wife, and about my friends. I read on.

> We have begun to discover that almost nothing that we were taught by our betters in or out of the architecture schools [and here I inserted, as I read, theological schools] of the mid-century has stood the test of time. Nothing—or almost nothing—turns out to have been entirely true (*RD*, May 1975, p. 163).

I let my mind drift back to that opening day on the campus of the Baptist seminary I attended in Ft. Worth, Texas. Fresh from college, I was eager to get started on my theological training. Wandering about the campus, I discovered the cornerstone on the administration building. There, chiseled in granite, was a portion of Scripture which was actually the motto of the seminary: "As ye go, preach . . ." (Matthew 10:7).

The Scripture verse, like everything else I had ever been taught, was incomplete. Unfinished. Where there should have been some kind of practical application, there was only an ellipsis, three dots signifying there was more, but that it wasn't important. Like all of us, the founding fathers were walking as best they could in the light they had. Their mistake came, perhaps, when they determined to chisel their theology—with all its incompleteness—in stone. As a result, a lot of us in that mid-century generation did the same as Peter Blake. We committed ourselves to a dogma in our youths which later turned out to be not entirely true. Like many of the others around me, I made the same commitment, only to find that when the rains came, my foundation crumbled beneath me. My theological house as well as my reputation and security—all fell.

Yet out of the ashes, like the fabled Phoenix, came a new being. It began with a dazzling experience I now recognize was the "baptism in the Holy Spirit," and has continued ever since. Almost at once I became aware that there was more to that ancient command of Jesus to His disciples than to simply "go preach." It was as though blinders had fallen from my eyes. I turned to the Bible and read with new understanding.

As ye go, preach, saying, the kingdom of heaven is at hand.
Heal the sick, cleanse the lepers, raise the dead, cast out devils; freely ye have received, freely give (Matthew 10:7, 8).

During those first years following my experience with the Holy Spirit, I mistakenly thought the "more" that I had discovered was limited to the sensational miracles found in the latter part of that verse. I was enamored with the "gift ministries:" healing the sick, raising the dead, casting out devils, et cetera.

Then gradually I began to realize that even more important than the command to heal the sick and raise the dead, was the message that "the kingdom of heaven is at hand."

There is more to Christianity than the experience of conversion, the experience of joining a church, the experience of the baptism in the Holy Spirit, the experience of deliverance from evil spirits. True, Jesus told His disciples that "signs and wonders" would follow their ministry, but it took me several years before I realized that statement was given to the disciples as a graduation address—and then only after three years of intense training in discipleship.

I have finally realized that the deepest hunger in the hearts of men and women is not to see miracles, but to enter the kingdom of God. Of course it is here that miracles abound, but to try to build a superstructure before the foundation is laid, always leads to disaster.

Unfortunately, even among those who are "walking in the Spirit," the commands of Jesus often go begging.

Love one another.
Be kind, tenderhearted, forgiving of one another.
Look not upon yourselves as better than others.
Walk the second mile.
Turn the other cheek.
Give with abandon.
Keep no score of wrongs done.
Lay down your life for the brethren.

Of such is the kingdom of Heaven.

Until we begin to walk in these simple commands, the real questions which plague us through life will go unanswered. Is it possible for me to be happy? Will I always scream at the children? Do I have to live with this lustful spirit forever? Why am I fat and miserable? Will I ever reach the place where I won't lose my temper with my wife? Why does my stomach get all knotted up when I think about that event in the past? Can I be healed so I won't withdraw in self-pity every time I hear the name of the mistress my husband used to keep?

The Holy Spirit came not only to comfort the afflicted, but to afflict the comfortable. Unfortunately, across the years many of us have become salt without savor, wine without ferment, rooted and rutted into our molds of immaturity and selfishness. We have grown comfortable, finding it easier to wear a mask than to permit ourselves to be seen by living transparently—and run the risk of being seen for what we really are.

That's really what this book is all about. Transparency. Openness. God knows I'm not there yet. The day before I sat down to write the final draft of this book I found myself in an argument with my wife. And because she didn't want to do the rather brash thing I had suggested, I stormed out of the room calling her a "stick in the mud."

There was a time I would have called her something a lot worse than that. And there was a time I wouldn't have admitted that we argued. I'm different than I used to be and I know that public confession of the truth about myself, and willingness to allow others to peer into my life and see my imperfections, are not only evidence of growth, but integral to the healing-growth process itself.

When the time arrived for me to type the final draft of this manuscript. Jackie and I agreed that the thing for me to do was get alone somewhere where I could work undisturbed. So, picking up my typewriter, notes, dictionary, Bible, and a ream of clean paper, I drove south to a motel along the highway where I ensconced myself in a small, sterile room overlooking an orange grove—and began to write.

The last day, as I was finishing the final pages, I heard a familiar knock at the door. It was the same young maid who had come in every day at the same time to change the bed and bring fresh towels. Always before she had worked around me, being careful not to bother the growing stacks of paper on the unused bed or disturb the various piles of notes lying on the dresser and tables. This day, however, she began to ask questions. Maybe she had never seen a writer at work, or maybe she figured I was about to leave. Whatever it was, that morning she was serious.

Her name was Debbie. At twenty-four years of age she was in the process of getting a divorce, although she was four months pregnant and supporting two other children at home. "My husband's hooked on drugs bad," she said. "He finally left me and the kids, so I had to get this job. You won't believe some of the stuff I have to take just to keep my job, but it's better than nothing."

She asked if she could sit down for a minute and rest. "It's hard to work when you're pregnant," she said. Then, looking over at me she blurted out, "You're a Christian, aren't you?"

I nodded.

"I thought so," she said. "I saw your Bible when I came in the other day, and I've been reading the stuff you've thrown in your trash can." Then her eyes filled with tears and she asked, "Do you think a person like me can ever be happy?"

So it's for Debbie, and all the others just like her, that this book is written. All those who are self-sufficient should stop here. The rest won't apply to you. But if you are needy, if your inner person is lonely, empty, and confused, then read on. Happiness *is* possible.

Remember, I'm talking about risky living. The kind that, if practiced, will turn your entire world upside down. But, what's the use of living if you don't attempt the impossible—even if it kills you.

1

DIVINE MADNESS

The question that continually bothers me is: Why am I not able to hear from God directly? Why is my channel always clogged? I want to hear from God, but I continue to stumble through life, believing that God has a perfect plan for me to fulfill, yet never quite getting there. At times I sense there is a great wall between me and the perfect will of God. Like Paul, the things I want to do, I don't do. The things I don't want to do, I am constantly doing. So I keep asking, is it possible to really hear the voice of God? And if so, is it possible to follow His direction?

It's easy for me to rationalize this and say, "The real problem in my life is my wife. If Jackie would hear clearly from God, then everything else would fall into place." But I know that is not the case. That's a cop-out. As much as I want her to hear from God, my real problem is me.

Every time I start down some path, I invariably come to a

fork in the road. It's at these forks of decision where I have my problems. I start, then I stop. I'm constantly backing up and starting over again, so that far more time is spent regrouping in confusion than marching forward in victory.

Now, after a number of years of going and coming, I have determined that the secret to hearing the voice of God is contained in Romans 8:5, 6. Here Paul says:

> *For they that are after the flesh do mind the things of the flesh; but they that are after the Spirit the things of the Spirit. For to be carnally minded is death, but to be spiritually minded is life and peace.*

A quick caution here. The word "flesh" in the Bible does not refer to your problem with overweight or lust. Those kinds of things only *result* from walking according to the flesh. But Paul is talking about a kingdom in which we live, a materialistic realm which puts wax in our ears and prevents us from hearing the voice of God, because, in that kingdom, we rule.

The Bible recognizes another kind of kingdom. A kingdom of the Spirit. In this kingdom God rules, and all who enter become His servants. They hear His voice and walk in His abundance.

Everybody who rules in his own kingdom is doomed to die. In fact, Jesus says they are dead already.

> *He that believeth on him is not condemned; but he that believeth not is condemned already (John 3:18).*

I vividly remember the afternoon a pretty, fifteen-year-old girl came into my study. Her world had fallen apart. She was pregnant. Rejected by her parents, she had taken the jagged edge of a Band-Aid can and had attempted suicide by lacerating the arteries in her wrist. Happily she was unsuccessful, but it

2

was indicative of her hopelessness. I talked to her, but I don't think she heard anything. She left, telling me that sooner or later she would again attempt suicide. She gave me a poem she had written. In four lines it collected the thoughts of a million lonely kids. It said:

These are the ones on whose tombs they'll inscribe:

"Died at fifteen, buried at seventy-five."
Out of the night we breathe a sigh
For those who are dead, but cannot die.

To live in the dimension of the Spirit is life and peace. To live in our own kingdoms is death.

Somewhere in this life, perhaps only in isolated areas, there are people who walk through this world exuding life and peace. They are surrounded by the problems of old age, poverty, sickness, grief, pain, hatred, and loneliness. Yet their spirit is a spirit of life and peace. No matter what comes at them, no matter what kind of catastrophe falls on their lives, inside they are filled with life and peace. They are like the rose petals which, when crushed, give forth beautiful perfume. Rare. Seldom seen. But they do exist.

God wants to bring us to that place. Yet we are worldlings. We are a people of reason and logic. We judge success by outward standards. We make our decisions on the basis of verifiable data: Is this course of action going to cost us money? Is it going to cost us reputation? Is it going to cost us popularity? As a result of our logical answers to these questions, we turn either right or left at the forks of our roads.

Last Christmas I had a long talk with our teenage son who was home from college for the holidays. Like many college students, he was always short of money. So, as fathers often do with children who handle money with reckless abandon, I called him aside for a conference. We sat on the side of the bed in an upstairs bedroom and our conversation went something like this:

"Bruce, you are spending too much money out there at school."

"But, dad, what's money for? Isn't it to spend?"

"Well, yes, son. That's the purpose of money. But you also need to save some for tomorrow."

"Is that what you're doing with the money you make?"

"Yes, we spend only as much as we need. The rest we save for the day when we won't have any earning power."

He just sat there looking at me. And the more he looked the more uncomfortable I became. I had a feeling he had been listening to my sermons on the joy of giving—and taking them literally. I slowly began to realize that I was saying to him, "Son, the time may come when God won't provide for you, and you'll have to provide for yourself. The *wise* man is one who stashes money away to meet this kind of emergency." Yet even as I spoke, I realized I was giving him the wisdom of this world, rather than the word of God.

We talked long that afternoon, and I received as much insight into God's plan for money as he did. Perhaps even more, as I realized how much I was depending on myself rather than God.

Plato, the Greek philosopher and a disciple of Socrates, said that there are three valid sources of knowledge. The first source of knowledge, according to Plato, is the five senses. We share these with the animals. We taste, hear, see, feel, and smell.

The second source of knowledge, according to Plato, is reason. Reason is the thing that sets us above all the other creatures. It enables us to reach a logical conclusion. It is this process that enables me to sit down and deduce, "Okay, I'm going to have fifteen more productive years during which I shall earn money. After that, my earning power will be greatly diminished." Therefore, on the basis of this premise I should begin to lay aside money for the time when the productive years will be over. Then I will not have to live off my children, who might one day come to me and say, "Daddy, you are spending too much money. You're going to have to cut down." There's nothing wrong with this kind of reasoning, but it can take you only a limited distance.

That's why Plato saw a third concept of knowledge. He called it "divine madness," referring to the entire world of spiritual communication. Here a man receives knowledge in a way which is neither through the senses nor through the mind. It comes from the Source of Power to our spirit. Some might call it *intuition,* others, *inspiration.*

Later, Aristotle, who was Plato's disciple, eliminated this third, or supernatural, source. He thought the entire intuitive faculty was invalid. Unfortunately, much of what we experience in the Western world is based on Aristotle's philosophy. We say if knowledge does not come through our senses or our reason, it is invalid. If we can't taste it, feel it, smell it, or if we can't deduce it, it is not real. Thus have we lost that vital balance which brings maturity to decisions based on knowledge received through the senses or by reason. In the Eastern and primitive cultures, references to the spiritual world abound. Dreams, visions, supernatural communication, talk of spiritual things—are common. Walk through the marketplace in Bangkok, Katmandu, or Manila, and everyone is talking about communication with the spiritual world. But for a man to use such language on the floor of the New York Stock Exchange, or in a board meeting at General Electric, would be sheer madness. Here in the West we rule out all talk of God giving us divine knowledge as poppycock. Oh, we believe in God, but we are unwilling to believe He can, or will, communicate to us through any means other than the senses and reason.

I do not believe God intends to destroy our reasoning

power. In fact, I believe He often uses it to communicate His purpose. In Isaiah 30, the prophet indicates that if a man is walking with God, he will basically walk by listening to his reason and following the five senses. However, if he steps off the path, or makes a wrong turn at the fork of the road, then he can expect to hear a gentle voice from within giving correction.

> *And thine ears shall hear a word behind thee, saying, This is the way, walk ye in it, when ye turn to the right hand, and when ye turn to the left (Isaiah 30:21).*

Now, we, in our Western idiom, call that "conscience." We would be much more accurate if we called it the "voice of God." But our "reason" forbids that. We know that if we stand in the marketplace and say, "God told me . . ., " we'll be laughed at. Therefore we opt for a cultural cop-out. Instead of saying, "No, I shall not do that because God forbids me," we grin and say, "My conscience would bother me."

I was amazed, during a visit to Thailand last year, to hear the wife of a high government official say at a luncheon, "The spirits commanded me to do a certain thing." I looked around at the military and political leaders who were present and saw they were all nodding their heads. They understood. But here in America we are unwilling to acknowledge the presence of God—or evil spirits. Why? Because we are *reasonable* people.

Reason causes us to say we should not act until we have full understanding. Until all the facts are in. But the Bible says that if we dwell in the secret place of the Most High (that is, if we are living in the kingdom of God), we shall abide under the shadow of the Almighty (Psalm 91:1). In other words, the closer we get to God, the more we walk by faith and not by sight.

The more you walk by faith and not by sight, the less you need to understand Him. Something else begins to happen. He takes over and directs your walk, your life, by divine intuition.

In Matthew 14 we read the story of Jesus walking on the water. When Simon Peter, the big fisherman, saw Jesus out there, he must have realized it was illogical. Peter had been raised on the water. He knew it was unreasonable for a man to walk on the surface. But when Jesus beckoned to Peter and said, "Come!" Peter forgot about reason. In a moment of spiritual exuberance, he threw his legs over the side of the boat and started out on the water himself—walking toward Jesus. It was not until his reasoning faculty began to work again that he sank. He had moved from faith to sight, only to discover that while Aristotle had grasped a portion of the truth, he had missed the better part.

Some of you have been there before. You started out in faith, but the closer you got to God, the darker things became. Then you backed off, reaching for the safety of the boat. "Boy, have I done a foolish thing," you think, as you head back to "safety." But had you gone on, you would have come into the actual presence of the Lord Himself.

In my little studio on the second floor of my house, I have an electric typewriter. If I were to come in one morning and flip the switch and not hear the familiar whirr, I would immediately look to see if my machine were plugged in. I wouldn't sit in my chair in front of the keyboard and wail, "Oh, electricity, please come into my typewriter and make it work." Nor would I bow my head in prayer and plead, "God, in the name of Jesus, fill my typewriter with power." No, I would simply plug the cord into the socket, which is the outlet for power, which in turn is connected with the source of power, and wait for the machine to begin to hum.

The entire universe is filled with the healing power of God. But in order to be healed, one has to come in contact with that power. God is the source of the power and the Holy Spirit is the outlet. Aristotle may call it invalid, and Plato may refer to it as "divine madness," but the Bible calls it the anointing of the

Holy Spirit. Without it we are powerless, ignorant, and left to our own devices.

God has made a world that is run by law—His laws. There are laws of nature, gravity, physics, chemistry, sound, and light. But there is another law—the law of love and grace—which supersedes all other laws. When God invokes this law, that is, when He intervenes in the affairs of men personally, we call it a miracle. But to God, such dealings are just as "natural" as an apple falling downward when it drops from a tree. Reason may say man cannot walk on water. But faith allows us to do the impossible.

Dr. Alexis Carrel, physician and scientist, declared that he had seen skin cancer disappear at the command of faith. That is not breaking the laws of nature. It is the superimposition of a higher law. If we were to investigate such healings we would always find that somewhere, someone along the line had reached down and plugged themselves into the available power—the power of the Holy Spirit who transcends all man's reason and senses.

There are millions of Christians who have died of disease whom God longed to heal. Countless others live on in misery and defeat because they are unwilling to pay the price of inner healing. God has provided, in the person of His Holy Spirit, the healing agent. All we have to do is reach out and touch Him.

When we are under the shadow of the Almighty, we are not walking by sight, but by faith. Yet it is here, in the shadowy place, that He covers us with His wings and gives His angels charge over us, to keep us in all our ways. It is here we find provision, protection, and joy—and healing. It cannot be reasoned out. It can only be accepted. By faith.

2

THE BLACK PIT

When you choose to follow Jesus, you voluntarily surrender the right to choose, or the power to vary, the consequences of that decision. From that time on, what happens to you is the responsibility of the one you voluntarily designated as the Lord of your life. It is His responsibility to direct the course of your life so you will eventually "be conformed to the image of his Son" (Romans 8:29). Thus every circumstance is part of God's design to bring us to maturity.

In his great chapter on maturity, the Apostle Paul says God is never satisfied with us until

> *We all come in the unity of the faith, and of the knowledge of the Son of God, unto a perfect man, unto the measure of the stature of the fulness of Christ: That we henceforth be no more children, tossed to and fro, and carried about with every wind of doctrine, by the sleight of men, and cunning craftiness, whereby they lie in wait to deceive; but speaking the truth in love, may grow up into*

him in all things, which is the head, even Christ (Ephesians 4:13-15).

I spent a night with my good friends, Dick and Betty Schneider, in their home near Morristown, New Jersey. I first met Dick at a writers' workshop sponsored by *Guideposts* magazine in 1967. Later Dick joined the staff of *Guideposts* and eventually moved up to the position of senior editor before he joined some of his former associates from *Guideposts* in a new publishing company.

As I was preparing for bed Dick came into my room and said a dear old friend of his wanted to meet me before I returned to Florida the next day. Since I needed to catch an early plane, Dick had invited him for breakfast. He promised me I was in for a pleasant experience.

Like many good editors, Dick underplayed his expectations. When I came down the next morning, I was greeted by a man who could have stepped out of the British Parliament. His name was Seabury Oliver. In his early seventies, his gray striped pants and conservative black coat gave the appearance of a man of refined taste and deep cultural origins. This, coupled with his slight British accent, made me wonder if the Schneiders had not imported him directly from Fleet Street.

Dick introduced Mr. Oliver as a financial consultant who had offices both in New York and in New Jersey. A widower, he was now semi-retired and living alone.

As we talked over Betty's breakfast, I soon realized that his spiritual heritage was just as rich as his business knowledge. An Anglican (naturally) by culture, he was attending the services at the First Christian Assembly in Plainfield, New Jersey, where Dick and Betty often fellowshiped. It didn't take me long to realize there was much I could learn from him.

During the course of our conversation I asked him how he came to know the Lord in such a deep, personal way.

He lowered his cup of tea and with a slight twinkle in his eye answered me in one word.

"Trouble."

Then he added, "How does anyone come to know Him?"

In one sentence he had summed up the heart of Paul's theology found in the eighth chapter of Romans.

For we know that all things work together for good to them that love God, to them who are the called according to his purpose (Romans 8:28).

In the jargon of the professional writer there is a term which describes that place in life when all the lights go out, when all our crutches are snatched away, when we physically, emotionally, and spiritually "hit bottom." The term is "the black pit." When a Christian writer interviews someone, he automatically begins to probe around looking for the black pit. When he finds it, he knows he has a story, for it is here that God has the best opportunity to speak in words we all can understand.

In Jesus' parable of the Prodigal Son, He tells about a boy who had everything his heart could desire, but was restless because he had to live under the authority of his father. He wanted to run his own life. Demanding his inheritance, he left home and "wasted his substance with riotous living." It's an old, familiar tale—common to all of us. After he had spent all he had, he learned his security had been in the wrong things. His friends disappeared as quickly as his money, and when hard times came he hired himself out to feed hogs—dipping into the swill in order to stay alive. For a Jewish boy, feeding hogs and having to eat their slop must have been the blackest pit of all. But it was here, for the first time, he saw himself as he was. Realizing how much better off he would be at home, he determined to go back to his father, admit his mistake, and offer himself as a hired servant. Leaving the hog pen he headed home, only to be welcomed by his father—not as a hired servant, but as a lost son who had been found.

Jesus told that story, not just to illustrate the tender love of the heavenly Father for all those who decide to come home, but to point out a principle of life. No man ever comes to inner healing until he has had the outer surface stripped away so the light of reality can shine on the impurities in the dark recesses of his life.

We cannot serve Jesus Christ on our own terms. We cannot insist that, if we follow Him, he must guarantee that certain kinds of things will never happen to us, or that certain other kinds of things must happen. Whatever method He chooses to shape our lives is His business, not ours.

I received some fresh insight into this when I attended a Camp Farthest Out (CFO) at Ardmore, Oklahoma. I was sharing the rostrum with a Methodist evangelist, Tommy Tyson, and a grand old Anglican Bible scholar, Estelle Carver. During one of the morning sessions Miss Carver, who was in her mid-eighties, was speaking about the gentle ways God uses to mold us until we begin to look like Jesus Christ. The more I listened, the more painful it became. It was as though God was attacking the canker sores in my inner nature with a sharp scalpel, scraping and cutting out the infection. On the verge of tears, I whispered to my wife that I had to leave the room. She reached over, squeezed my hand, then released me. She understood.

It was early April and the wind whipping off the water of Lake Murray was sharp and chilly. The little white clouds scudding through the sky seemed to match the frothing whitecaps which lashed the rocky shore. Wanting to be completely alone, I walked out on the long wooden dock and sat cross-legged, my back against a large piling which gave only partial protection from the biting wind. It was one of those incisive times when a man doesn't want warmth and security, but needs to expose himself to the elements as well as to the searching finger of God's Spirit—the *ruach* (or wind) which was the Old Testament word for the Holy Spirit.

Almost at once a Scripture verse came to mind.

> *Looking unto Jesus, the author and finisher of our faith (Hebrews 12:2).*

I had read this verse many times and always envisioned the writer talking about the spiritual qualities of Jesus. "Author and finisher" had always seemed synonymous with the first and the last, the alpha and the omega, the beginning and the end. But now I saw it with a fresh understanding. Jesus was a carpenter, and these were carpenter's terms. Author meant creator, architect, the one who drew the plans and nailed the thing together. Finisher was also a carpenter's term. The man who does the finishing work on a piece of furniture is the fellow who works with sandpaper, smoothing and polishing until the creation reflects the face of the creator.

That's what Jesus was doing to me. In fact, that's what He had been doing ever since that summer's night back in 1953 when I turned my life over to Him. As I reflected, I could see that everything that had happened to me since that time had been designed by God to finish me, to bring me to the place where I was conformed to the image of His Son.

In 1950, after having been members of churches for a number of years, after having raised their children in the best traditions of morality and ethics their humanistic backgrounds afforded, my mother and father had a dynamic conversion. Daddy was already in his sixties and was considered by the members of his church and his business associates to be a dedicated churchman—and thus a Christian. However, his Christianity was cultural rather than personal. It took a black pit experience for him to reach that place the Prodigal Son reached when he came to himself. His conversion, along with Mother's, was dramatic and life-changing. Almost at once they began to concentrate their efforts on their blacksheep son—me.

It took three years before I finally gave in and agreed to accompany them for a week during the summer to a place called Word of Life Camp on an island in Schroon Lake in the Adirondack Mountains of New York State. One night, during a campfire service, an invitation was given asking those present who had never made commitments to Jesus Christ to come forward. I was hesitant, shy. When the others stepped forward, I hung back. However, after all the others had returned to their rooms, I lay under the stars, watching the sparks from the fire drift heavenward, and surrendered my life to Christ. I did not want to be as one of those sparks which burned brightly and then died to fall back to earth as dead ash. I wanted to be like one of the stars which burned forever. I asked Him to take my life.

I didn't know it then, but I had surrendered the right to choose or the power to vary the consequences of my decision. In the fifth book of the law, Moses laid down an unerring principle concerning the nature of God. He always requires our vows of us.

> *When thou shalt vow a vow unto the Lord thy God, thou shalt not slack to pay it: for the Lord thy God will surely require it of thee; and it would be sin in thee (Deuteronomy 23:21).*

One of the reasons there are so many unhappy Christians is they have never understood this principle. They feel God should do them favors, heaping them with material rewards and benefits, rather than working as a carpenter to shape their lives back into His own image.

My own black pit came in the fall of 1967. After a series of failures in the ministry, I was almost ready to give up on organized Christianity as irrelevant, a force without power, salt without taste. I had signed a contract to write my first book, *Run Baby Run,* the life of a young Brooklyn boy from Puerto Rico, Nicky Cruz, who had been converted under the street ministry of David Wilkerson of *The Cross and the Switchblade* fame. But even the excitement of becoming a professional writer did not ease the nagging feeling that there was something missing from my life. For several months I had been hearing stories of miracles happening in some corners of Christianity, but it all seemed so elusive, so far away from where I stood culturally. I knew Jesus and His followers laid hands on the sick, even the dead, and saw them restored. But I was unable to relate that to our modern, sophisticated type of Christianity which was confined to church buildings and church programs. I was on the verge of chucking the whole thing as impossible when God broke through in a dramatic way.

In November of 1967 I met with Nicky Cruz to begin my research on the book. My publisher, Dan Malachuk, a New Jersey businessman, had just established Logos International. *Run Baby Run* was his first major book, and he encouraged me to interview Nicky on his own turf—the streets of Brooklyn.

It was a cold, rainy afternoon when Nicky, Dan, and I came down the stairs in the old Teen Challenge building on Clinton Avenue in Brooklyn. In the vestibule we found our way blocked by a heroin addict, a "junkie," who had dragged himself in out of the rain and lay retching and moaning on the stairway. As we stepped around and over his shivering body, Nicky reached out and laid his hand on the back of the man's head. I watched in silence. That anyone would touch such a miserable creature was a shattering experience, especially since his head was full of open, running sores. But it wasn't the fact that Nicky prayed for the man, it was how he prayed—in a strange, unknown tongue. It lasted only a few seconds, and then Nicky moved on.

I had never heard tongues before, always believing it was some kind of "trance-talk." How well I remembered the time when I was a seminary student in Ft. Worth and the students and faculty were all atwitter about some of the people in a Baptist Church in nearby Handley, Texas, who were reportedly "speaking in tongues." The reaction ranged from "tsk-tsk" to "that's heresy." But this wasn't heresy. It was power. Within seconds the junkie ceased his heaving, groaning, and shaking. Laying his head over on the steps, he simply went to sleep. Attendants from Teen Challenge helped him up the stairs to a bedroom. I learned later he had been completely delivered from dope in those few seconds.

But it was the few seconds that "blew my mind." Something had happened. Something spectacular. It was as though God had come down and surrounded us in the vestibule of that old building in Brooklyn.

Nicky and Dan walked on outside, laughing and talking, leaving me behind dumbfounded. Shaking myself loose, I finally caught up with them. We stood in the freezing rain on the sidewalk while I gasped breathlessly, "Didn't you see what happened back there? That prayer was answered instantly!"

I was not accustomed to instant answers. Dan looked at me strangely and said, "Don't you Baptists believe God answers prayer?"

It was not a fair question. Baptists do believe God answers prayer. And so did I. It was just that I had never seen it happen in such a dramatic fashion

After we got in the car and headed back toward New Jersey where the Logos offices were situated, I recalled something J. B. Phillips had written in his Translator's Preface to *Letters to*

Young Churches, his modern translation of the Epistles of Paul in the New Testament. Phillips said of those early Christians:

> Perhaps if we believed what they believed, we might achieve what they achieved.

Was this so? Had I actually seen the "works of Jesus" carried out by a Puerto Rican kid who could hardly speak English, or was it some kind of illusion I had manufactured because I wanted to believe it so badly?

The secret, Dan told me, was an experience called "the baptism in the Holy Spirit."

There followed three months of arguing with myself and with anyone who dared mention the subject of the supernatural power of God. I was afraid, I now realize, to completely turn my intellect and emotions over to God—afraid He might cause me to do something foolish. As long as I was in control, I wouldn't do anything foolish, but if God was in total control could I really be sure? Yet, it was this element of self-control that had brought me to the edge of despair, had thrust me into the black pit. In reality, I was far more out of control than I cared to admit.

Three months later I met Nicky again for our second interview. I flew to Washington, D.C., to attend a regional convention of the Full Gospel Business Men's Fellowship International (FGBMFI). Nicky was to speak at the youth meetings and it was a good opportunity to spend some more time with him.

Something happened to me that weekend in Washington. It was the beginning of an entirely new life for me. It took me several months to adequately evaluate the experience, and even then I was still too awestruck to arrive at any firm conclusions. But one thing was certain. I was not the same man.

I returned from Washington on a Saturday, and on Sunday morning, February 25, 1968, I met with the small band of people who made up the little Baptist church I was pastoring in Melbourne, Florida. All my life I had been afraid to go into the pulpit without first having written out every word I was going to say. But that morning, without notes, I stood before the people and shared from my heart. The following is a word-for-word transcript of what I said.

I am not sure how you will receive what I am about to share with you. It could be construed as the words of a man gone completely insane—or the words of one who has witnessed and experienced the power of God in an awesome way. I shall leave the evaluation up to you.

Last Monday night I attended a prayer meeting held in a school building in Arlington, Virginia. It was made up of businessmen from many churches in the Washington area. [Actually this was a group called "New Adventures in Prayer" which met under the supervision of a businessman named Jack Zirkle. After more than ten years the meeting is still going with large numbers of people from the Washington area in regular attendance.] There were more than six hundred present. I was dumbfounded at their enthusiasm and freedom of worship. They sang with great intensity, and when they prayed many of them raised their hands. The service was punctuated with shouts of "Praise God," "Amen," and "Thank you, Jesus."

The next afternoon I went with Nicky and a local businessman, Al Malachuk [Al is the brother of Dan Malachuk and has for many years been active in the Washington FGBMFI] to the U.S. Naval Academy at Annapolis where Nicky addressed a group of Christian midshipmen. I sat back in amazement as these young middies and their officers shared in the time of testimony. There was no timidity. They spoke boldly of the changing effect of Jesus Christ on their lives. Many of them testified of having been "baptized in the Holy Spirit." I was especially impressed with the testimony of a young naval aviator, Lt. Commander Bob Wright, who was overflowing about the power of God in his life.

Wednesday night I had my first experience with the Full Gospel Business Men. Al Malachuk chaired the meeting which was held at the huge Shoreham Hotel. I was amazed that they had no formal order of service. They said they were "following the leadership of the Spirit."

I had reservations about my participation in the meeting, fearful those attending would be fanatical in nature. But they weren't. They came from all kinds of churches—Methodist, Presbyterian, Baptist, and Episcopal. I was especially interested in the large number of Roman Catholics present, many of them priests and nuns. Al introduced me at the meeting and I spoke about five minutes, telling about the book and the testimony I felt the book would have. However, I was very ill at ease. The people seemed genuinely interested in what I was saying, and when I finished they clapped in approval.

I took a seat on the front row while the other guests were introduced. During the early part of the service, Al came down off the platform and whispered in my ear that he felt "led by the Spirit" to ask me to sing a solo. I was dumbstruck. I enjoy singing, but this was a new experience to me. Al returned to the platform after telling me that as soon as the introductions were finished I should come forward. I had no music and my mind had gone blank. I couldn't even remember the words to the Doxology. I made my way around to the organist and asked if she had any music. She was playing by ear. Even the organ bench was empty. By this time Al was motioning for me to come to the microphone. About to panic, I frantically told the organist to begin playing "How Great Thou Art." I sang the first verse and the chorus and could remember no more. In desperation I asked the congregation to join me as we sang through the chorus again. They did. My, how they did! They came to their feet singing with more enthusiasm and joy than I had ever experienced in my life. They forgot all about me, and with arms raised toward the ceiling and tears running down their faces, they sang, "How Great *Thou* Art." I was deeply moved and almost staggered off the stage to my seat.

The next afternoon I attended a Bible study led by David duPlessis, a South African with a traveling ministry. There were more than 2,000 eager people present, most of them with Bibles and notebooks. I stood next to the wall of the crowded ballroom, carefully observing the people present.

My eyes were drawn to a beautiful young woman sitting on the end of a row. She looked like a fashion model. As we sang "Amazing Grace," she raised her hand—just one delicately gloved hand—and there was a radiance on her face like I had never seen before.

Directly in front of her was a little, stooped man. He must have been ninety years old. He was bent and feeble, but as we sang, "When we've been there ten thousand years," he raised his head and the same radiance was on his face. He held up both arms as far as they would go, not much past his chest, and with tears streaming down his face, sang about the glory of heaven. I was so overcome I could hardly breathe.

Something special was going on. Where did this freedom come from? Where did they receive the power to lose their earthly inhibitions? I had to find out.

After the meeting I cornered an Episcopal priest who had been on the platform. I felt that I would be safer talking to a man with a clerical collar. He agreed to have dinner with me in the dining room prior to the evening service. I confessed I was afraid of these strange people who "spoke in tongues," yet I needed some answers.

That night, at the dinner table, we openly discussed this experience known as the "baptism in the Holy Spirit." I had a growing feeling I was familiar with what he was describing, only I had always referred to it as "total commitment" or "surrender." Yet as we talked, I realized this was not something you did—it was something you received.

- "But didn't the Holy Spirit come into me when I accepted Jesus as my Savior?" I asked.

"Yes, in fact, without Him you could not have accepted Christ. Paul says: 'No man can say that Jesus is the Lord, but by the Holy Ghost' (I Corinthians 12:3). However, there is more."

The priest went on to illustrate his point. "I own an ocean-going ship," he said. "Aboard this ship I have a twelve-man life raft. It is bulky, heavy, and contains a cartridge of compressed CO_2. If I throw it overboard in that condition, however, it will sink. It *contains* the CO_2 (Spirit) but it is not *filled*. Only when the release is pulled does the gas fill the raft, blowing it out to the size and shape for which it was made. That's what the Holy Spirit wants to do to you. He's in you, now He wants to fill you."

I was still having trouble. "There's no such thing as a second experience," I said, quoting some of my former professors.

Much to my embarrassment, he pushed back the dishes on the table, and while those around us looked on, he produced a huge black Bible. He opened it to Acts 9 and very deliberately read me the story of Saul's conversion on

21

the road to Damascus. However, he added, three days later the Holy Spirit sent a man called Ananias to lay hands on Saul that he might "be filled with the Holy Ghost" (Acts 9:17). I saw, but was afraid.

He asked me what I thought of Mark 16. I told him I simply ignored the last few verses as something I couldn't understand. He asked me if I believed the Bible was true. I said yes. Then he said, "Why don't you believe these passages?" I had no answer. He asked if I believed that Peter, John, Philip, and the others actually performed miracles. I said yes. He said, "Do you think God can still perform miracles through His people?" I recalled the experience on the steps of the Teen Challenge building in Brooklyn. Yes, I believed that also. Then he asked the clincher: "Has He ever performed a miracle through you?" I had no answer.

After supper we hurried back to the main assembly hall. There were more than 3,000 people present. The meeting had already started and the only seat left for me was on the third row directly in front of the preacher.

The meeting began with a series of testimonies. Judge Kermit Bradford from Atlanta told of the amazing power of God which changed his life. A priest from Notre Dame told of receiving the Holy Spirit and later speaking in tongues. Several businessmen gave similar testimonies. All said this new "infilling" allowed them to witness and praise God without restriction.

All around me people were smiling, clapping, and saying, "Praise God," right there in public.

Then the moderator said, "Let's be quiet and listen for a word from God." The assembly got unbelievably quiet. It had been noisy before, not bedlam, but a warm, friendly noisiness. Now it was still.

Suddenly from the far back I heard a voice. It was the

most beautiful, melodious speaking voice I had ever heard. I knew it was an "unknown" tongue. Yet it wasn't babble. It was ecstatic. It sounded like some American Indian dialect. The voice spoke in sentences with voice inflections which indicated punctuation. The speaker continued for about a minute and then stopped.

Immediately a man four seats down from me on the same row began to speak in the first person with the most authoritative voice I had ever heard. He said:

I have sent you and anointed you to preach. I shall never leave nor forsake you. I shall be with you always. You will be great in the kingdom of God because it is my Spirit that leads you. The task is great and many are lost, but in my Spirit you shall overcome.

I was overcome. As he spoke I stood trembling, choking back the tears. I had the awesome feeling that this was God's message to me—alone. That out of all these 3,000 people He was speaking to me, the skeptic.

We sat down and I felt that anything else that followed would be anti-climactic. I was embarrassed over my emotional condition, but no one else seemed to notice. The experience of having had a "word from God" was so strong I could hardly contain it. I wanted to stand back up and shout, "He spoke to me," but I didn't dare. I had the feeling that if I did, everyone in the room would have shouted, "Praise God," or something like that.

They introduced the preacher. He was John Osteen, a Southern Baptist from Houston, Texas, a graduate of Baylor University and Southwestern Baptist Theological Seminary. It was, without doubt, the greatest sermon I had ever heard—yet all he did was share his testimony. I identified with everything he said. He told of how he had longed for additional power in his ministry. How he felt that God had intended him for greater things than a denominational box. How he recognized the superficiality and powerlessness of all his church activities. He told of seeking this power, yet being afraid to receive it. After he received this "baptism in the Holy Spirit," he began preaching and ministering with new power. He told of one service in India when he put his hands on blind people and they literally received their sight. It was fantastic.

At the close of his message he gave an invitation for any who wanted to accept Christ to come forward. About fifteen did, and he prayed for them right there. Again I was impressed. Everything was definitely Christ-centered.

Then he called all those who wanted to be "baptized in the Spirit" to come forward. Hundreds responded. I began to feel terribly uncomfortable and wanted to leave the room, but I couldn't get out. I was trapped in the mob of people milling around the front. Some of them were praying, some crying, some laughing, and others speaking in tongues. I kept reminding myself I was there as a writer, I wasn't supposed to get involved. But I was involved. I was right in the thick of the action and couldn't get away from my chair because of the crush of the crowd.

I decided to sit down and wait for things to thin out so I could leave. I put my head on the back of the chair in front of me and suddenly began to cry. I was crying so hard I could hardly catch my breath. It felt like all the dams inside had burst and I was being flooded from within.

I felt someone bump me as he sat down beside me. I tried to look up, but couldn't. I was blinded from the tears. Then I recognized the voice of the Anglican priest with whom I had eaten dinner. I could sense he was praying for me. I tried to get him to stop, but he kept right on. I was sobbing, "No, no, no, no." I wanted to turn loose, but was afraid, still bound to this earth and its kingdoms.

Then I felt an arm go around me from the other side

and heard another voice praying. He was asking God to baptize me in the Holy Spirit. I had never gone through such an intense emotional turmoil. I knew that if I turned loose God would take all the things I held precious, leaving me helpless, totally dependent on Him. I struggled to hang on, but was crying so hard I could no longer object.

The priest moved around in front of me and put his hand on my head. When he did, something snapped loose inside of me, in the vicinity of my heart. For a split second I wondered if I was going to die. Then I didn't care anymore. A great peace swept over me, as though God had taken His hand and wiped away the tears.

I looked up to see who was on the other side. It was Commander Wright, resplendent in his dress uniform, his chest full of ribbons. How he had spotted me in that mob of people I will never know. Here were the only two men in Washington I respected enough to have reached me—and God had put both of them beside me there in the black pit.

That was back in 1968. I closed the testimony that morning saying: "Whether I'm mad or not, time will tell, but I have the feeling that something inside me has been healed. For the first time in my life I feel like a 'whole' person."

The lights had been turned on in my black pit.

3

LORD OF THE SUBCONSCIOUS

It was on a Sunday morning, almost four years after that remarkable experience with the Holy Spirit, that I became aware of the healing work which had been going on in my inner man—and the tremendous need I had for more. I awoke at my regular time that morning, then realizing I could enjoy the luxury of a few minutes of extra sleep, deliberately turned over and buried my head in the pillow.

As I slept, I dreamed. It was a typical dream—inane, senseless, and composed, I think, of various people from my childhood parading back and forth engaging in foolish activity. It lasted only seconds and then was gone.

I awoke and realized I had been dreaming another of my nonsensical dreams. Most of my dreams are like this. One recurring dream has me slogging my way through a gooey swamp. I am up to my knees in thick mud. Each step is laborious and I am panting for breath. Behind me, almost ready to catch up with me, is some kind of monster that is gliding along the surface of the swamp with ease, ready to pounce on me. Fortunately I have always awakened just before he wrapped himself around me.

I seldom give any thought to my dreams, but this morning, standing in the bathroom shaving, I began to run a quick self-inventory.

"Why is it, Jamie, that you never dream of spiritual things?" This bothered me since some of my more spiritual friends were always talking about the great revelations that came to them while they were asleep. They dreamed about angels, cherubim, heavenly hosts, and even about Jesus Himself, while my dreams were confined to faceless monsters chasing me through a swamp.

It bothered me, especially since I was beginning to have a deeper walk with God during my waking hours. Dreams, I knew, are the reflections of our real selves. They are, for the most part, the mirror of our souls—the conscious revelation of the subconscious part of our selves.

If the mind were pictured as a deep mountain lake, the consciousness would be the surface and the subconsciousness all that lies beneath the surface. The surface not only reflects all that is around it, but it acts as a receiving point for everything that enters. Except for the contour and capacity of the basin (heredity), everything that is in the lake has been put there (environment) through the conscious. Some of it stays on the surface where it can be seen, but the vast majority of all our experiences have sunk—or been pushed—into the depths of the subconscious.

Everything that has happened to us, from the moment we were conceived in our mother's womb, is part of that vast reservoir called the subconscious. Most of the unpleasant experiences have been pushed under so we can maintain a relatively calm and pure surface appearance. Yet deep inside, often forgotten yet still very real, lie the painful, traumatic experiences that make up a big part of our real selves.

As the conscious mind goes to sleep and relaxes, items from the subconscious—that great storehouse of suppressed material that involves the larger part of the mind—come floating to the surface—much like bubbles rise to the surface of a lake. Often they actually break out into the open, mixing with the conscious mind in sleep, causing us to dream.

The same process takes place when the conscious pain-sensitive mind is put to sleep by an anesthetic. Sodium Pentothal (sometimes known as ''truth serum'') is an anesthetic used to put the conscious mind to sleep artificially, allowing the subconscious, under the direction of an authority figure or some stimulus, to respond to facts long stored beneath its surface.

When I was a junior in high school I dislocated my elbow during an afternoon football practice. My father and mother went with me to the emergency room of the local hospital where our family doctor, E.B. Hardee, tried to manipulate the arm back into its socket. It would not budge.

"I'm going to give you a shot," Dr. Hardee said. "It will put you to sleep for a few minutes and while you're asleep, I'll adjust your elbow."

"Uh, what kind of shot?" I asked.

"Sodium pentothal," the doctor answered, preparing the needle. "Now I want you to begin counting backwards from one hundred and . . .''

"Just a minute, doctor," I said, trying to get up from the stretcher. "Isn't that the stuff they call 'truth serum?' ''

He grinned and nodded his head. "You've been reading too many detective thrillers," he said.

"Won't that stuff make me say a lot of things I might not ordinarily say?" I asked. Like all high school football players, I had been exposed to some pretty raunchy language, and had engaged in some of it myself. Not only that, but I had a lot of other junk down inside I didn't want exposed, especially in the presence of my mother and father.

Dr. Hardee approached me with the needle. "Don't worry, son," he said gently. "You won't expose anything that's not already in your mind."

I felt the sharp prick of the needle in my arm and remembered drifting off to sleep saying, "That's what I was afraid of."

My parents (bless them) never did say whether I revealed any deep, hidden secrets. They didn't have to. I knew I was capable of it just the same.

Back when I was sixteen it didn't seem very important that my lake was filled with garbage. But now, having made an open profession of faith in Jesus Christ, and having put on all the outward trappings of a Christian, I was concerned about my double life. On the surface I certainly looked like a Christian: I spoke the language of Zion, I controlled my tongue and actions. But down inside I knew I was a cesspool.

In the twelfth chapter of Luke, Jesus talks about the "leaven of the Pharisees, which is hypocrisy." He is actually describing each one of us who spends time cleaning off the surface of our lake, but is not willing to pay the price of dredging the garbage from the bottom.

As I stood looking in the mirror that Sunday morning I realized I had given considerable time and effort to keeping the surface of my lake clean. My conscious mind, to the best of my knowledge, was dedicated to God. Yet at the same time I realized that much of me was simply a reflection of those around me. In fact, rather than have someone ripple the surface of my lake and therefore reveal what may be lurking beneath the surface, I found myself often agreeing with everything other people said. That way my surface remained calm, peaceful. Yet all the while, inside, I was a cesspool of disagreement and impurity.

How easy it was to agree with the preacher in church. As I left I would shake his hand and say with a wide grin, "Great preaching, brother!" This kept the surface of my lake unruffled.

But once in the car I would reveal my true self.

More and more, on the surface, my lips were speaking praises to God and my life was showing forth the image of Jesus simply because I willed it to be. But my subconscious, that vast reservoir of who I really was, that area revealed primarily through dreams and sudden disturbances of the surface, still seemed to be as un-Christlike as ever.

That same morning at church I had another vivid illustration of just how devoid of spiritual things most of my subconscious actually was. I was in the process of growing a beard, and it was just beginning to take on some kind of personality of its own, looking less and less each day like I had smeared peanut butter on my face and wrapped my jaws in briers. I was standing in the vestibule of the building, talking to one of the elders, when an old friend, Allen Reed, walked up and with a practical joker's look, reached out, grabbed a pinch of whisker under my chin—and yanked.

I reacted violently—with a clenched fist. He danced back, laughing and pointing to my fist, already up in a fighting position. "Scratch the surface of the lamb and find a wolf," he chuckled, much to my embarrassment.

I was chagrined, not that I had reacted (for a man will always react to pain), but that I had reacted with closed fists. Allen had broken the surface of my consciousness and revealed a Christless area where self reigned supreme.

I sat in the back of the room that morning, half-listening to the teaching and half-reflecting on how much my life was out of tune with God's perfect harmony. I remembered how I had reacted the day before in the parking lot of the grocery store. I had come out of the store with my arms loaded with hamburger buns for a cookout. A pretty girl had driven up in a sleek sports car and was wriggling out from under the steering wheel. As she did, her skirt slithered up beyond the point of propriety and suddenly I was suffused with lust. It was stupid. I had no intention of being immoral, especially not there in the grocery store parking lot. But the glands of my body were suddenly activated. On the surface I was God's man of faith and power. Underneath I was a dirty old man.

That afternoon, still smoldering from the revelation of my "dead-men's-bones-character," I spent some time on the patio helping my teenage son, Bruce, build a wooden gate to fence off our garbage cans. He was holding one end of a board while I nailed. During the process he accidentally moved the board just as I was bringing the hammer down. The result was catastrophic. The hammer glanced off the side of my thumb, peeling the flesh. This disturbed the surface of my lake, and roaring out of the muck and goo on the bottom of my subconscious came an expletive I hadn't used since those high school football days.

I looked up at Bruce and his eyes were wide with amazement. Never, not in all his seventeen years, had he heard his daddy say such a word. And with such vigor!

I quickly regained my composure and apologized. "I'm sorry, Bruce. I don't know *where* that word came from."

But I did know. I knew when it had entered my life and who had put it there. I also knew that I had pushed it under the surface of my lake, hoping it would never reappear again. But it had. The stirring of the water with the head of a hammer had been just the right stimulus to bring it forth.

For the most part I had been able to keep my overt reactions under control. (One of the fruits of the Spirit is self-control.) But it bothered me that beneath the seemingly calm and tranquil surface of my life there lay that seething mass of self that was for the most part materialistic, animalistic, carnal, and only slightly flavored with the Christ who had seeped down from the conscious surface into the dark, hidden areas of the subconscious.

In less than twenty-four hours I had seen evidence that even though my consciousness was under control, my subconscious was still quite capable of fleshy acts. It was not a pleasant revelation.

Not everything that lies beneath the surface of our conscious mind is so easily identifiable. Carol Mull, the wife of the county fire chief in our community and a deeply spiritual person, told me of an incident that illustrates the kind of problem that affects all of us. The Mulls' daughter, Cindy, had married a young airman, Dave LeBeau. They were stationed at McDill Air Force Base in Tampa, Florida, and lived in an apartment building with several other couples.

Cindy was eight months pregnant when the apartment building caught on fire. Dave was at the base and she had been resting when she smelled smoke. She rushed out and found the flames already roaring down the hall. Since her daddy was a fireman, she knew the danger and went from apartment to apartment, frantically warning others and making sure all the children and animals were safe. Several fire trucks answered the call and they finally pulled Cindy from the building, assuring her everyone was safe.

Everything they had was destroyed, and Dave and Cindy moved in with friends in the church. They stayed there until after the baby, a little girl named Michele, was born. However, it wasn't long before they began to realize that Michele seemed to have an inordinate fear of loud noises. Especially was she scared of sirens and would look wide-eyed with fright whenever she heard one. Fortunately, her parents knew something about the necessity of inner healing. They began, at an extremely early age, to lay hands on her and pray for her. As she grew older, Dave took her out to the base and showed her the fire trucks. When they came to visit Cindy's parents, the Mulls would let her sit in the fire chief's car. Whenever they heard a siren they would love her, comfort her, and pray for her. She's two years old now, and even though she still has a vestige of fear of loud noises, she is rapidly being healed of that wound which scarred her life even before she was born.

Realizing that we are a composite of all the experiences we've ever had, the Freudian psychoanalyst spends much of his time digging into our past, our subconscious. He may use drugs, hypnotism, or other forms of therapy to help bring the latent problems to the surface. However, once they have been exposed, the most the secular psychoanalyst can do is help us "adjust" to our condition.

There is a vast difference, however, between adjusting to the wounds of the past and having them healed. I still remember the sensitive young man who belonged to a rival fraternity when I was in college. He had strong homosexual tendencies and on the advice of a counselor, sought psychiatric help. After a number of sessions the doctor finally told him he would be a lot happier if he learned to adjust to his gay life. Three weeks later the boy shot himself.

The average man lives behind a mask. His smiles, his laughter, his piety, his shows of confidence are all part of the role he is playing. Seldom, if ever, does he let anyone know who he really is. Only in times of pain, fear, or perhaps when he has had too much to drink, does his mask come down and we see him as he really is.

For thirty-five years I wore a mask and was largely unaware of it. I didn't like myself, and was continually imitating someone who seemed successful (never dreaming tnat he, too, was probably wearing a mask). As a minister, if I heard of some program or activity that was "working" in some other church, I could hardly wait to get it started in mine. I tried to sound like Billy Graham when I preached, like Bev Shea when I sang, and like Cliff Barrows when I made "announcements." I wanted to be all things to all men that I might be thought "winsome."

Always, though, my mask was up. I dreaded the thought of someone peeking behind it, seeing the real me, and rejecting me. Afraid of growing bald, I considered a hairpiece. Afraid I would not be known as an "effective" speaker, I memorized the sermons of several successful men of the cloth. I knew God wanted me to take off my mask. To be open. honest, and transparent. But the fear was too great. It was almost strangling me. What if people discovered I was nothing more than a shell, the lid on a garbage can? Would they still love me? Still respect me? I thought not. The things I had buried were, I knew, unacceptable. I had rejected them. Why wouldn't others, if they discovered the awful truth?

A friend of mine says the best way to disarm your critics is to confess publicly ahead of time. This way no one can ever accuse you of something you have not already confessed. But what do you do when you have so much to confess—so much garbage in your lake?

I began to get some insight into who I really was when I realized that my life was, on the whole, a reaction to stimuli.

It had been several years since I had been to Ft. Worth, Texas, where my wife and I spent the first four years of our married life. Flying to Dallas on a business trip, I decided to rent a car and drive over to Ft. Worth on a nostalgia trip. With the construction of the new turnpikes, the highways between Dallas and Ft. Worth were unfamiliar. Coming into Ft. Worth, I found myself in one of those multi-level interchanges called a "mix-master." Knowing that if I got off on the wrong road I could be swept off towards Oklahoma, I slowed down, carefully studying my map and paying close attention to the big green highway signs that loomed overhead. Suddenly I was jolted by the blast of an air horn from behind. Looking up into my mirror, I saw a lumbering old dump truck almost touching my rear bumper. The driver, snarling, was leaning on his horn. No doubt he had seen my out-of-state license plate and was disgusted that some foreigner was blocking his Texas highway.

I reacted. Out of my lake came roaring all kinds of thoughts. My first thought was to slam on my brakes. I knew that rear-end accidents in Texas were always charged to the following driver. That would teach him a lesson or two, even if it demolished my car. My next thought was even worse. I considered throwing my map out the window, hoping it would spread across his windshield, causing him to swerve off the road and crash onto the next level of highways, far below.

Fortunately, my conscious mind took control and pushed the thoughts of hatred and murder back into my subconscious. I motioned him by and turned off at the proper junction toward my destination. But it didn't end there. For the next ten miles I fumed. I enjoyed chewing the cud of what I could have done. I even half-heartedly wished another dump truck would blow his horn at me. This time I had things all planned out.

You see, the driver of the dump truck had suddenly taken charge of my life. My stomach was in knots, my lips dry, my breathing shallow. All because I had given in to a reaction, rather than responding positively in love.

Moving from the area of reaction to the area of positive response is one of the most difficult of all spiritual tasks. In order to do so, the reservoir of the subconscious mind must be cleansed, dredged out. The Bible says we were made in the image of God. This is our true heredity. Yet our nature has a penchant to sin. And rather than dealing with our unhappy experiences as they have happened, we continue to push them beneath the surface of our lake. Thus when the surface is broken, instead of revealing the form of God the Father in whose image we are made, we reveal our wounded, angry selves.

We try, so bravely, to cover up. We stoically push the hurts deeper and deeper, or we cover them up with a nervous giggle or a smear of piosity. Yet deep inside we're still the same. Unredeemed. Real healing will always include a healing of these memories. This will allow us to begin to become transparent so that any rift in the surface will reveal, not ourselves—which is an accumulation of the old wounds, disappointments, and fears—but the heavenly Father.

Jesus was able to do this. Jesus was transparent. That is the reason He was able to say to Philip, "He that hath seen me hath seen the Father." Jesus never called men to look at Him. He said He had come to reveal the Father. The way He did this was through perfect transparency. There was no muddy water in the subconscious mind of Jesus. He never blurred the image of the Father by reacting.

Unfortunately, we are not like this. When the surface of *our* lake is peeled back, we "show ourselves" rather than revealing the Father.

Perhaps, though, we can at least understand what Jesus meant in the Sermon on the Mount when He said, "Let your light so shine before men that they may see your good works, and glorify your Father which is in Heaven."

For years I had been concerned about what I called the "curse of ancestry." Every medical examination called for a series of questions on my ancestry. Has anyone in your family died of cancer? Did your father have heart disease? Diabetes? Is there a history of insanity or epilepsy?

I have a godly father, a man who deeply loves the Lord. He has provided a heritage rich in culture and deep in the things of the Spirit. I am grateful. But he is still a man with human frailties and physical disabilities. And according to the Bible, I do not have to remain a slave to my ancestry. One of the most fascinating promises in the Scriptures tells me that through Christ I can actually die to my old ancestry and become an heir to God and a joint heir with Christ. No longer do I have to be in bondage to the fact my father had diabetes, or my mother had high blood pressure. When I became a new creature in Christ, old things passed away, all things became new (2 Corinthians 5:17). This means I am now the inheritor, not of my earthly father's liabilities, but of the assets of my heavenly Father. John, talking about Jesus, said that "as many as received him, to them gave he power to become the sons of God" (John 1:12), and Paul indicates that the whole creation is standing on tiptoe, waiting to see who will be the first to step forward as a "manifested son of God." That's exciting. But it will come only as we allow the Holy Spirit to permeate our entire being, claiming it for Christ.

Paul was talking of this when he wrote:

> *For though we walk in the flesh, we do not war after the flesh: (For the weapons of our warfare are not carnal, but mighty through God to the pulling down of strong holds.) (2 Corinthians 10:3, 4).*

Most of our warring, or battles with self and Satan, are on the conscious (or fleshly) level. The Bible commands us to be holy people. Therefore, to achieve holiness, we try to clean up the surface of our lake. We cut out smoking, try to lead chaste lives, stop gambling, cut our hair (if we're men) or don't cut our hair (if we're women), wipe off the facial makeup, lower our hemlines, raise our necklines, and go through a hundred different mechanical procedures trying to achieve holiness.

But Jesus didn't call this holiness. He called it hypocrisy, because the inner man was still polluted. Such battles, Paul says, are not to be fought on the surface level. Holiness is not attained by cleaning the surface of the lake. This battle must be waged on a spiritual level, which is the reason that any sincere study of inner healing needs to include a study of spiritual warfare.

Several months ago I spoke at a Full Gospel Business Men's meeting in Morristown, New Jersey. Before the meeting, a group of men asked if I would join them and pray for a young housewife named Elizabeth who had been brought to the meeting on a stretcher. Tumors in her hip bones had progressed to the point where she could not bend her body into a sitting position. She either had to stand up or lie down.

We prayed and, as is often the case, she experienced a dramatic healing. In fact, the very next day she was able to drive her car for the first time in many months.

Several months later I was back in the Morristown area and called her on the phone. She was discouraged. Although her body still showed evidence of the healing, she was coming under strong attack from some unlikely places.

When the minister of her church discovered she had been healed, he told her she could no longer take a responsible role in church activities. It was evident he feared she might testify of her healing. He was unprepared to handle this kind of "fanaticism." In fact, he told her, it would be far better if she just dropped out of church completely.

This wounded not only Elizabeth, but her husband, who was not a Christian and had a serious drinking problem.

"I don't want to feel bitter and resentful toward my minister," she said over the phone. "But I can't help it. What can I do?"

It was obvious to me that the battle was a spiritual battle. The minister, unfamiliar with the healing aspect of God's personality, was not striking out at her. He was striking out at the unfamiliar. He opposed anything that might threaten the security of his ministry. Unfortunately, in the process he had literally become the devil's advocate. Therefore it was extremely important that Elizabeth not give in to her natural feelings, but neither should she try to hide them. The battle was being fought in the heavenlies, as though it was being waged over her head. Satan had found a cooperative warrior in the form of the minister, but if she tried to battle Satan in her own strength she would surely lose. I told her about the archangel Michael who was the one God usually sent to do battle against Satan. And since he was the one who would do the actual fighting, all she had to do was keep herself transparent so the minister could see the image of God at the bottom of her lake.

When she saw this, she was greatly relieved. The attack was not against her. In fact, it was not even coming from the minister. The minister, in this case, was merely the devil's advocate. She, in turn, should be Christ's advocate. Thus all she had to do was reflect the character of Jesus and let the angels fight the battle for her. The last time I heard from her, she had done just that. In fact, she had grown stronger spiritually since she now realized it was not up to her to do the fighting.

In this same Corinthian passage Paul goes ahead to say that the way to come into complete inner healing is by

Casting down imaginations, and every high thing that exalteth itself against the knowledge of God, and bringing into captivity every thought to the obedience of Christ (2 Corinthians 10:5).

Our reactions lurk beneath the surface of our lives, waiting for a chance to pop through. Our job is not to run busily over the surface of our lake making sure none appear, but to let them come, see ourselves as we really are, confess the sin, thank God for the cleansing and ask Him to change our heart.

Impossible, you say. Yes, if we try to fight the battle on the surface of the lake. But if we let the Holy Spirit go to work with a sieve, not just pulling down the imaginations but dredging them up, then we can see that transparency is possible.

I determined that was what I wanted for myself. Not only to reflect Christ on the surface of my life, but deep down in the subconscious areas as well. I was tired of looking at the mushrooming pornography appearing all around us and being forced by my reactions to think lust. I knew that I could spend the rest of my life trying to fight that battle on the surface—with both blue laws and cold showers—and never win. I knew there had to be a place where I could enter so deeply into the kingdom that even when I was surrounded by pornography and vulgarity I would, instead of looking upon a woman to lust after her, see in that naked body the very image of God.

I was tired of being pinched and reacting with a closed fist, of feeling myself flare up when someone blew a horn at me, or biting back the curse words when I hit my thumb with a hammer. I was tired of finding tender places in my life where the veneer was so thin that if I were scratched I revealed vast, unhealed areas of self-pity, prejudice, and resentment. I wanted to be Christ's to the core. I wanted Him to be the Lord of my subconscious.

But how?

We were getting ready to build some upstairs rooms on our Florida house. Before we could actually start the construction, however, the builder wanted to test the soil around the base of the foundation to make sure it could take the additional weight. He didn't want to run the risk of having the house tilt or the floor crack as the earth settled.

One Monday afternoon a team of geological engineers came by the house. They had a clever kind of drill that punched a small hole in the earth, going down about twenty feet and coming back up with samples of the various layers of soil. They discovered that the surface sand was only about three feet deep. After that it changed to marl (which is a sandy type of clay), then shale, and finally bedrock. They concluded the soil could easily stand the additional weight of the second story.

After they left I stood in the yard and looked at the soil samples they had dumped out on the grass, wondering what would happen if someone should take a similar boring of me. Despairingly, I concluded that although they would find Jesus Christ in great abundance on the surface, in the deep areas of my life they would find only me.

Yet my desire was that such a drilling would reveal Jesus Christ all the way down to the bottom. I wanted to be so pure that when I was cut, I would bleed Jesus. I thought of that story in the seventh chapter of Acts where Stephen was stoned. The Bible says the surface of two lakes were broken that afternoon. Stephen's words to the religious leaders cut them to their hearts. What was revealed? Hatred, bitterness, and murder. They reacted so violently they dragged Stephen through the city streets and stoned him to death. Yet as he was cut with the stones, Stephen, instead of reacting, responded with such positive love that eventually one of those involved in the stoning, a Pharisee named Saul, was converted.

I wanted to be like that. But how could it be? My lake, it seemed, could never be free from pollution. I was learning to handle the junk that was falling into it on a daily basis—but what could I do about the dregs which had long since settled below the surface and rose only in times of stress, anger, or temptation?

In other words, was it possible (as Paul commanded in Romans 12:2) for my mind to be actually transformed to prove what was that good, and acceptable, and perfect will of God? The Scriptures said that I was "predestined to be conformed to the image of His Son" (Romans 8:29), but by what method was this to be accomplished? "Walk in the Spirit, and you shall not fulfil the lust of the flesh," Paul said to the Galatians (Galatians 5:16). A similar promise was made to the Ephesians "That he

42

would grant you, according to the riches of his glory, to be strengthened with might by his Spirit in the inner man; that Christ may dwell in your hearts by faith'' (Ephesians 3:16, 17). Again he said, ''Put off concerning the former conversation the old man, which is corrupt according to the deceitful lusts; and be renewed in the spirit of your mind'' (Ephesians 4:22, 23).

So what I desired was not an impossibility. In fact, it was to be the goal of every follower of Jesus Christ. Being made conformable to His image would not begin with an outward expression, however, but with the healing of the inner man (the subconscious). In other words, the best way to clean up the surface of the lake was not by skimming the top, but by purifying the source of the flow from the wellsprings at the bottom.

Still the question remained: How is this brought to pass? I saw several scriptural principles that applied.

First, the Christian must be committed to a walk of absolute obedience to Christ in his *conscious* life. He must stand guard at the doorpost of his mind to repel each evil thought by which Satan would gain entry. Also, he must hurl out those he finds already inside, in the name of Jesus. The Bible says the Lord will honor such obedience with a cleansing of the heart. But if the Holy Spirit is to have completely free access to minister to all corners of the subconscious, He must be invited in.

It was there I discovered the full meaning of Paul's phrase, ''pray in the Spirit.''

For years I had heard people talk of the benefit of ''praying in tongues.'' In fact, I myself had a ''prayer language'' which came as a result of being baptized in the Holy Spirit. But I had always used the prayer tongue simply because the Bible said I should. ''I would that ye all spake with tongues'' (1 Corinthians 14:5). Now I began to understand there was a purpose for the prayer language other than simply obeying God.

In 1 Corinthians 14:4, Paul said, ''He that speaketh (prays)

43

in an unknown tongue edifieth himself.'' Now that's what I needed, to be edified—to be strengthened— in my spirit, in the deep areas of my subconscious. In that same chapter he said, ''If I pray in an unknown tongue, my spirit prayeth even though my understanding is unfruitful'' (1 Corinthians 14:14). It was beginning to make sense.

About that time I made a visit to Peru to interview members of the Wycliffe Bible Translators about their jungle aviation program. The first man I came in contact with in Lima was a noted linguist with several Ph.D. degrees in linguistics. Before I could ask any questions concerning my mission, he said, ''Do you pray in tongues?''

I was taken aback, not expecting even to get into this subject. However, I quickly recovered and told him that I did use a prayer language in my private devotions. He was greatly excited. ''I've been wanting to talk to someone about this for a long time.''

He went ahead to say that, as a linguist, he was constantly having to filter words through his intellect before he could speak them. ''Every sound I make has to come through my mind,'' he said. ''As a result, I am always polluting my prayer life with my thoughts. For a long time I have longed to be able to pray, to commune with the Father without having to think about the words—simply letting the Holy Spirit who is in me bypass my intellect and go directly to the Father who is in heaven. Is that what tongues is all about?''

I had never thought of it that way, but as I heard it from the lips of this distinguished linguist, I realized that was it— exactly. Not only that, but by praying in tongues I was actually inviting the Holy Spirit to come into my spirit, to enter my subconscious, and bring the purity of the heavenly Father with Him. It was a tremendous revelation.

While I was in Peru I restudied this entire concept of inner healing, especially in the light of Romans 8. In verse 26 of that chapter I ran across the secret of how to bring into captivity every thought to the obedience of Jesus Christ. Here is what Paul says:

> *Likewise the Spirit also helpeth our infirmities; for we know not what we should pray for as we ought: but the Spirit itself maketh intercession for us with groanings which cannot be uttered.*

I had always viewed this verse as an explanation of intercessory prayer—the prayers we pray for someone else. But as I read it over again during my stay in South America, I came to a new understanding. Simply by changing the pronouns from plural to singular I understood.

> Likewise the Spirit also helpeth *my* infirmities; for *I* know not what *I* should pray for as *I* ought; but the Spirit itself maketh intercession for *me* with groanings which cannot be uttered.

Paul was talking about praying in the Spirit, whether it was in tongues or by letting the Spirit make intercession with groanings which could not be uttered. In so doing I would invite the Spirit to abide in my subconscious. Even though the prayer would be meaningless to my understanding, I knew His presence would eventually bring my every thought into captivity to obedience to Jesus Christ. No wonder Paul said we should pray without ceasing. To cease would quench the Spirit and block our inner healing.

Now I can see where the sick areas of my mind, including the bad memories of the past, can actually be healed as the timeless Christ walks back through my past and touches with healing; or as He descends far beneath the conscious surface of

45

my mind into the hell of my own creation and preaches the good news of deliverance to those thoughts so long held in captivity. As I pray in the Spirit (and for me that means using my prayer language), those areas of my subconscious where self has always sat on the throne are brought under subjection to the King of the mind, Jesus Christ, revealing even my subconscious to the One who "searcheth the heart and knoweth what is the mind of the Spirit" (Romans 8:27).

I recalled an incident that began two days after I experienced the baptism in the Holy Spirit. I had returned from Washington, D.C. with a new honesty. It was an honesty that compelled me to confess—to my wife—events which I had for years pushed beneath the surface of my lake in a vain attempt to keep them hidden. Now came a desire to be transparent, and a knowledge that this could only transpire as I got things out in the open.

The following night, after this long confessional period, I began to dream. In my dreams I relived many of the carnal activities of prior years. People I had not thought of for years appeared in my dreams—people I had manipulated, despitefully used, lied to and hurt. Night after night they paraded through my dreams, helping me relive in vivid detail all the immorality and evil manipulations of the past.

I was mystified. Why, after I had just gone through this deep purification process, was I now having to suffer through this. The only other Spirit-baptized person I knew of in our community was a former minister with the Church of God, Anderson, Indiana. Elbert Jones had been dismissed from his church and was now ministering to a small interdenominational group meeting on Tuesday nights at the Women's Club building. Later he was to become one of my closest friends and would serve by my side as a fellow minister in the local body. However, at this time he was a virtual stranger.

Desperately needing help, though, I sought him out and asked if he could give me some kind of explanation for my bizarre dreams.

He smiled and said, "The Holy Spirit is busy dredging up the junk in your subconscious, letting it float to the surface."

"But what can I do with it?" I asked.

"Rebuke it," he said matter-of-factly. "It is floating to the surface because the Holy Spirit is now moving actively in the deep areas of your mind, stirring the waters, so to speak. When you rebuke these memories of the past you not only cast them out, but you close the door on the areas where they first came in."

I followed his advice, and have continued to do so ever since. In about two weeks the dreams ceased, and even though I am aware that my lake is still polluted, I realize it is being purified by the fresh water that wells up from that free flowing fountain in my inner being. As a result, even my dreams are beginning to take on spiritual overtones—and, on occasion, I even hear from God while I am sleeping.

Thus the baptism of the Holy Spirit, rather than being a climax to the Christian experience, is simply the door through which the Holy Spirit entered my subconscious. Eventually He would "fill" me. And when that happened, well, even before it happened, I would find the mirror of my soul, my dreams, beginning to reflect the condition of my subconscious. Eventually I would dream, not about monsters and swamps, but about Jesus.

4

PRAYING IN THE SPIRIT

The other morning, just at dawn, I was driving north along the deserted ocean highway between Vero Beach and my home in Melbourne, Florida. The highway follows a strip of sand and trees which separates the Indian River, which is actually a salt-water lagoon extending along the east coast of the state, from the Atlantic Ocean.

Suddenly my little Volkswagen was atop the high bridge over the Sebastian Inlet. On one side the blue of the Indian River shimmered toward the mainland, barely visible on the western horizon. On the other side was the magnificent sunrise, exploding out of the emerald green sea in a kaleidoscope of color that was so awesome it literally took my breath away.

Early that morning I had read from the Living Bible. Now the words of David burst spontaneously from my lips: "Hallelujah, yes, praise the Lord! Sing Him a new song!"

I remembered the words of the grand old hymn I learned as a boy in the First Baptist Church of Vero Beach:

Holy, holy, holy, Lord God Almighty,
Early in the morning my song shall rise to Thee.

But even this was not sufficient to express the explosion of adoration that came rushing from my soul as I longed to worship, to praise Him in the ''womb of the morning.'' My human vocabulary was too limited, too restrained.

I pulled off the highway, up a little sand road to the top of a dune overlooking the ocean, and cut off my engine. For long moments I sat in silence, feasting my soul on the miracle of God's new day. Then, from the very depths of my inner being, I heard the Holy Spirit Himself begin to speak, praising the Father through my lips. I was speaking in the language of the angels.

It was an unforgettable moment. Sheer ecstasy. And long after the sun had risen like a great fireball, dragging behind it the heat and light of a new day, I sat in the front seat of my little car, looking out beyond the crashing surf, praising God in the Spirit.

Praying in tongues was not a new experience for me. Although it was not the "initial" evidence of my baptism in the Holy Spirit, I do believe I received the gift at that time (even though it was more than two years before I appropriated it) and believe it is surely for all believers—regardless of whether their experience with the Holy Spirit is similar to mine or not. However, using tongues to praise God was new. Wonderfully new.

I remembered, shortly after experiencing the baptism of the Holy Spirit, that I shared my testimony before an interdenominational group. A visiting pastor, angered by what I said, approached me after the meeting. "Even if tongues are for today," he snapped, "what good are they?"

I was disturbed by his defensiveness, for although I did not speak in tongues at the time, I believed it was a valid gift of the Spirit. But I was equally disturbed that I could not answer him intelligently.

"All I know is that Paul says he spoke in tongues more than all the others," I answered, "so it must have been of some value to the Christian."

He snorted and walked off, leaving me frustrated. I believed some things were to be accepted on faith alone. But I also agreed with my friend that there was a difference between toys and gifts. Toys are to be played with. Gifts used. I didn't believe God would give us "gifts" unless He had a solid purpose for each one.

It was in the two years following my baptism that I began to discover His purposes. It started with a growing desire to appropriate this gift into my devotional life. Shortly after I received the baptism in the Holy Spirit, my wife, Jackie, wakened me in the middle of the night, walking through the house laughing, crying, reading her Bible, and praising God. A week later she made a special visit to the home of a local Baptist minister, Bob Johnson, to ask his wife, Woody, to pray with her about speaking in tongues. She knew the Johnsons had been "praying in the Spirit" for some time and was eager to receive all God had for her too.

Woody later told me what happened that morning when Jackie came to the house. After they prayed, she said, they got up and began walking around the room, their hands raised as they praised God out loud. This was new for Jackie. Like myself, she had been raised in a Southern Baptist church, and of course for the last fifteen years I had been her pastor as well as her husband. According to Woody, the more they praised God, the more they were aware of His presence. They were experiencing the truth of David's psalm: "O thou that inhabitest the praises of Israel" (Psalm 22:3).

Then, without warning, Jackie's language changed. Instead of walking around the room saying, "Praise God, Hallelujah, I love you Lord," she was simply saying "La-la-la-la-

la.'' Again it was reminiscent of an Old Testament experience prophesied by Isaiah and later referred to by Paul in his letter to the Corinthians:

> *For with stammering lips and another tongue will he speak to this people (Isaiah 28:11).*

Jackie returned home that afternoon ecstatic with joy. I suspected she had spoken in tongues, but was reluctant to quiz her about it. Even though I had reached the place in my spiritual growth where I could give credence to the gift, I was still fearful. The scars of the past when I had formerly equated the ''tongues speakers'' with the ignorant people of the community who couldn't control their emotions were still with me. Even though I saw the tremendous difference the exercise of the gift made in Jackie's devotional life, I was still too proud to reach out and appropriate it for myself.

My problem was aggravated one afternoon when two women came by the house. I had been working hard on the final draft of my first book for Kathryn Kuhlman, *God Can Do It Again*. Jackie was out of town and the children were in school when I answered the door. I knew the women. They had attended our church and some of the home meetings. One was a Pentecostal evangelist and the other the mother of one of the young couples in the church.

They immediately got to the point. ''God has sent us to pray for you to receive the baptism of the Holy Ghost.''

''But I had that experience last February,'' I said.

''We've heard your testimony,'' the evangelist said, ''and praise God for the wonderful change in your life. But you haven't received the baptism in the Holy Ghost, because that's always accompanied by speaking in tongues. You need the gift of tongues.''

I was open for anything the Lord had for me. Even though I

was certain that God had touched me with His Spirit, re- volutionizing my life, I didn't want to quench His Spirit. If these women had a "word from God" I was ready to listen.

They wanted to go back to my study so we wouldn't be disturbed by the phone. After asking me to sit in a chair, they began marching around the little room praying loudly in tongues. The walls echoed, almost shuddered, with their prayers and praises. All this time I sat in the chair with my head bowed, beginning to feel a little uneasy, yet not wanting to miss a blessing if God had something special for me.

The praying turned to prophesying. Through the din I could hear first one woman, then the other, crying out, "Thus saith the Lord." They laid hands on my books. On my typewrit- er. They prophesied over the picture of an airplane hanging on the wall. They sang, chanted, laughed, and cried. But they never laid hands on me and, to my knowledge, never prayed for me specifically. This lasted for almost half an hour and finally, in exhaustion, the woman who was the mother of the young couple in our church said, "We've done what we were sup- posed to do. It's time to go."

I bid them goodbye and they left through the back door. I sat back down in the same chair, filled with wonderment. What in the world was that all about? They said they came to pray for me to receive the baptism of the Holy Spirit, yet they never did. Had God revealed something to them? Did they realize, as they prayed, that I had indeed been baptized in the Spirit? Or, did they discern something about me that was so filthy and un- worthy that I was unqualified to receive any gift from God? I never did find out what happened that afternoon, but somehow it seemed to be related to the work of the Spirit in my life.

That summer Jackie, the children, and I spent a month in our little mountain cabin in North Carolina. We often vacation there, enjoying the fresh mountain air and the unhurried atmos- phere of rural life. Art Katz, a young Jewish Christian, had joined us the week before, and I was spending most of the daylight hours working with him on the manuscript of his book, *Ben Israel*. At night Art and his wife, Inger, were staying in the nearby village, leaving our family alone up on the mountain.

Combining what was supposed to be our vacation with my work had put considerable strain on our family relationships. One night, after we had gone to bed, Jackie and I had some kind of disagreement. I don't even remember what started the argument, but I have no trouble remembering how self-righteous I felt about it. This book had been ordained by God. It was critical we get it out as soon as possible. Jackie had no right to criticize me for taking time away from less important things (like being with the children) to work on the manuscript. On and on we went, neither one of us stopping long enough to actually hear what the other was saying.

Frustrated, I finally threw back the covers in the dark bedroom and said, "Maybe you'd just like me to leave."

Jackie grew very quiet. She knew, after living with me for all those years, that I had reached the boiling point.

"Answer me!" I said through gritted teeth, not wanting to wake the children who were sleeping in another part of the house.

She said nothing, and in exasperation I stormed out of bed, grabbed my trousers, and pulled them on over my pajamas. "I can't stand this anymore. Here I am trying to do the work of God, and all I get from you is criticism."

I started out of the room but paused at the door, waiting in the darkened hall, hoping she would respond. In the darkness I could see the form of her body on the bed, still, motionless. Snorting, I walked through the living room, felt my way through the dark kitchen and out the back door into the chilly night air. I let the door close with an audible click and then waited outside the house, hoping that Jackie would follow me, entreating me to return to bed. But the house was silent. Suddenly I realized I had played the part of the fool.

I glanced around. It was past midnight and the grass and small rocks under my feet were wet with dew. I shivered in the cool air. The heavy woods behind the house were silent. Even the frogs and crickets had gone to sleep. And here was I, God's man of faith and power, sulking around in bare feet and pajamas, hoping my wife would come outside and beg me to return to bed. I was mortified.

My pride was too great to let me go back inside immediately, so I turned and walked down the familiar path into the woods behind the house. I had walked that path every summer since I was eight years old. I knew every stump, the location of every poplar, white pine, hickory, and laurel bush. The woods were dark and deep, hushed. I reached a junction where the path goes down the hill to a small brook and paused, looking up through the towering trees at the stars overhead.

"I've made a fool of myself," I told God out loud. "Forgive me."

There was no answer, but deep inside I remembered those strange ladies who came by the house, saying I needed to speak in tongues.

"Is that why you have me out here in the woods in the middle of the night?" I asked aloud. "Do you want me to speak in tongues?"

Again no audible answer, but once more, deep inside, I heard an inner urging that said, "Get down before me."

"Is that what it is going to take?" I thought. But without hesitation, for I was learning then to be obedient to the still, small voice, I dropped to my knees on the moist leaves which carpeted the forest path. I fully expected to break forth in tongues, but there was nothing.

Again the inner voice said, "Get down before me." This

time I started to protest. I did not relish the thought of prostrating myself on the ground. Even though the frogs and crickets had gone to sleep, I knew the little creatures that lived under the leaves were still very much awake—and crawling around. But the urging did not diminish. "Get down before me."

"If that's what it takes to speak in tongues, then I'm ready," I said. Without further hesitation, I spread myself flat on the ground, face down, arms extended. I was as low as I could get. I waited, expecting a torrent of sounds to come tumbling from my lips. Nothing! I waited for a long time and gradually began to feel like a complete idiot. I rose, brushed myself off, and returned to the house. It never occurred to me that God had been talking about a condition of my soul—pride—rather than a physical position when He said, "Get down before me." That revelation would take a full nine months before it was ready to be born.

Slipping back into the house, I got as far as the living room, but my pride once again blocked the way. I simply could not go back into the bedroom, for to do so would mean admitting defeat. Jackie had won. Actually, she had been right all along, and my explosion of childish anger was simply the shield I had thrown up to keep from being exposed. I eased myself onto the couch in the living room, resigned to spending the night there, covered with old newspapers and throw pillows to protect me from the chill of the mountain night, rather than in my warm bed.

As I got quiet I heard, coming faintly from the bedroom, the sound of Jackie praying in tongues. Her voice was soft and melodious. She knew I was out there, shivering, my teeth chattering, my pajamas covered with wet leaves, too proud to come into the bedroom. And she was praying for me. It was almost more than I could take, and I turned my face to the wall and wept my way to sleep.

That seed, planted, unknown to me, by the Holy Spirit that

night, grew slowly during the next nine months—much as a fetus grows in a mother's womb. I completed *Ben Israel* and started to work on a book for Pat Robertson, *Shout It From the Housetops*. My publisher encouraged me to visit Pat at the Christian Broadcasting Network offices in Portsmouth, Virginia, and later to drive up to Washington, D.C., to attend the regional convention of the Full Gospel Business Men's Fellowship International. Since my initial experience with the Holy Spirit had been at one of these conventions, I eagerly accepted his invitation.

The second afternoon of the convention was billed as a "Miracle Service." Kathryn Kuhlman was to minister and since I had grown to appreciate her, working closely with her on *God Can Do It Again,* I made plans to attend the meeting. I had been feeling woozy that morning and skipped lunch. I didn't think much about it, but as the Kathryn Kulhman meeting got underway I began feeling worse. I kidded with myself, saying I would probably be the first person in history to attend a healing service and get sick. But get sick I did. In fact, I got so sick, feverish, and nauseated, that I finally staggered out of the ballroom in the Washington Hilton and made my way to the elevator and up to my room.

I was too sick to undress and just fell across the bed. One moment I was burning up with fever, the next I had pulled all the covers around me as I shivered in a bone-rattling chill. I was aware it had grown dark outside, but I was too sick to switch on a light. Sometime, during the afternoon, I kicked off my shoes, but I remained fully dressed, moaning under the covers.

About six o'clock I picked up the phone and asked the front desk if there was a doctor on duty. The clerk said the doctor had gone home for the day and would not be back until ten in the morning. I hung up, thinking it would be too late by then. I had never been so sick in all my life. In my delirium I faced the possibility that I might be dying. I was too sick to care.

Off and on, as the night dragged by, I heard myself praying. I begged God to "do something." I knew I could call my publisher who was staying in the same hotel, but I hated to disturb him in the middle of the night. I finally reached the place of saying, "God, I've written a book on healing which tells all about your healing miracles. But I've doubted whether what I was writing was true or not—even though I have seen the evidence. Now I need to be healed. I've been too proud to ask you for anything, but I'm asking you, now, to touch me."

Then, softly, coming up out of my subconscious, I remembered that night on the damp leaves of the forest floor in North Carolina. And I heard God saying, "Now, you're down before me."

I began to pray again, but this time, instead of English I heard different sounds coming my my lips. Strange sounds. They seemed almost oriental in nature, without the nasal inflections. I was praying in tongues.

Several weeks before I had attended a Don Basham teaching seminar on the Holy Spirit at the Eastminster Presbyterian Church in Melbourne. In his lesson on speaking in tongues, Don had suggested it might be a good idea to write down, phonetically, the first sounds you spoke in tongues. As I prayed, his words came back to me. Still deathly sick, I crawled out of bed and, on my hands and knees, made my way across the carpet of the darkened hotel room to the coffee table in the middle of the room. There, on a small notepad, using only the light that filtered through the window blinds, I printed out, phonetically, the sounds that were coming from my mouth.

"Ya-she-ka-see-ma-tee-lay-moe-tuu-shan."

Leaving the pad on the table, I crawled back into my bed. With some satisfaction I thought, "Now, when they find my corpse in the morning, they will also find that pad. My Pentecostal friends will be satisfied. They will know I died speaking in tongues."

But I didn't die. In fact, as the night wore on I began to feel better. I dozed, and each time I awoke I was speaking in tongues, saying those same words over and over with new joy and power.

Sometime, just before daylight, I had an encounter with Satan. "You're just making that up," he said. "It's a product of your fever and delirium. Anyway, that's not tongues, that word you're saying is the name of your Japanese camera."

I listened, and sure enough, the first word, the most pre-dominant word I was speaking, did sound like *Yashika*. But the battle was already won, and Satan's tactics failed. I dozed off to sleep saying, "Even if it is the name of my Japanese camera, I'll say it to the glory of God."

When I awoke it was mid-morning. The sun was streaming through the windows. The little pad of paper was still on the table. The words were still tumbling from my lips when I prayed. And I was healed.

Had the language been the babbling sounds of a delirious mind? No, I believe it was the Holy Spirit praying through me, taking over and uttering words which my delirious mind could not handle. I believe it was the kind of praying referred to in Romans 8:26:

> *Likewise the Spirit also helpeth our infirmities: for we know not what we should pray for as we ought: but the Spirit itself maketh intercession for us with groanings which cannot be uttered.*

Besides, if it had been simply delirious babbling, it would not have continued. Yet it has continued, for years, and its use has grown more precious and meaningful each day of my life.

It was another year before I discovered the value of praying in the Spirit for inner healing. Our family was sharing a vacation cottage on the outer banks of North Carolina with Judge Allen

Harrell, his writer-wife Irene, and their six children. One morning after the women and children had taken off for the beach, the judge and I sat on the porch and talked. It was one of those special times when two men expose their souls to each other.

I had been intrigued with the concept of my subconscious being the composite of all my experiences, the mountain lake idea discussed in the last chapter. "How do I purge my inner self of the garbage I have collected across the years?" I asked Allen.

In his eastern North Carolina drawl, the judge told me: "I hold court in several cities. Each morning when I leave the house and drive out of town, I use the time in the car to pray or sing in the Spirit. And you know," he chuckled, "God is using this to cleanse me, to purify my soul."

It was his testimony which led me to discover something of the tremendous purgative, cathartic purpose of praying in the Spirit. There is a deep healing that goes on in the subconscious as one prays "in tongues." Down there, in the deep areas of the mind, as the Holy Spirit communes with the Father, old hurts are dredged up and healed, inherent character flaws are replaced with supernatural strength, and the carnal nature dies to take on the nature of Jesus. It is what Paul refers to in Romans 12:2 when he talks about the transformation that takes place by the "renewing of your mind." Once again I saw the beautiful practicality of this gift which edifies (builds up, strengthens) the believer.

Is the gift of tongues for the church today? Of course, just as much as are the gift of prophecy and the gift of healing. But as with any gift, it is to be administered under the authority of the church government and should at all times be for the building up of the entire body.

Is tongues the initial evidence of the baptism in the Holy Spirit? Not necessarily. In my own case it was more than two years after I received the baptism in the Holy Spirit before I spoke in tongues. There are several places in the New Testament where men received the baptism in the Holy Spirit and there is no evidence they immediately spoke in tongues. Such was the case with Paul in Acts 9. However, we later find Paul saying he speaks in tongues "more than ye all." Therefore I have to conclude that tongues is not the evidence, but the consequence of the baptism in the Holy Spirit.

Is it proper to seek the gift of tongues? From my own experience, and from a study of the Scripture, I have concluded that any time we seek anything less than the kingdom of God we are asking for too little. That is not to say God will not honor a person's sincere desire to receive a prayer language in order to praise and intercede with fullness. But when Paul outlines all the gifts of the Spirit in 1 Corinthians 12, he finishes the chapter by saying that all do not have the gifts of healing, all do not speak with tongues, and all do not interpret. These are gifts that God divides "severally as he will" (1 Corinthians 12:11). However, Paul says, we should covet earnestly the best gifts.

What is the best gift? Some might say it is love. But love is not a gift, it is the *way* in which the gifts are to be manifested according to 1 Corinthians 13. The best gift is the person of the Holy Spirit Himself. This leads me to the conviction that I am not to seek the gifts, but the Giver. Once I receive Him into the inner places of my life, once He comes to transform me by the renewing of my mind, once He becomes the Lord of my subconscious as well as my conscious mind—then whether I speak in tongues is immaterial, for I shall speak whatever He wants.

Perhaps I can best illustrate this by telling you a couple of personal stories. Several years ago I flew to Colombia, South America, to begin my research for *Into the Glory,* the story of the pilots and mechanics of the Jungle Aviation and Radio Service, the flying arm of the Wycliffe Bible Translators.

My old friend, Tom Smoak, had flown me deep into the jungle to a small Indian village. We landed our single-engine plane on a tiny airstrip only to learn the chief of the tribe had been taken by canoe and river launch to a hospital in an upriver town.

The chief's old wife, fearing her husband was dying, was preparing to leave that day by canoe to see him. It would take her three days of paddling to reach the town. We could fly her there in twenty minutes, and offered to do it.

Tom helped her into the back seat of the plane and strapped her down. All the time she kept speaking in her language and gesturing outside the plane. She wanted her grandson, a half-naked nine-year-old child, to come with her. He was standing outside the window of the plane, tears making little streaks in the dirt on his face.

Tom patiently explained that we were at maximum weight and any additional weight would mean the plane could not clear the towering trees on takeoff. The chief's wife understood, but the little boy, standing under the wing, continued to cry and beg to go along.

Something in me let me understand how he felt. His grandfather, the chief, had been taken away, maybe dying. Now his grandmother was strapped in the back of a strange silver plane that would roar off into the sky. Panic, terror, fear, and loneliness—I could read it all in his eyes as he huddled against the fuselage, wetting the plexiglass window with his tears.

I stepped out of the cockpit and bent over, putting my arm around his bare shoulders. I heard myself praying softly in tongues. It lasted only seconds, but when I finished, the child turned and looked in my face, his eyes filled with wonder. Pulling away, he ran to the edge of the grass strip to join the other Indians who had come out of the village to watch the takeoff. We taxied to the end of the strip, gunned the engine, and released the brakes. As we roared into the air, I saw the little boy clutching the skirt of an Indian woman and waving at the plane—his face wreathed in smiles.

I have no idea what I said, or what the Holy Spirit prayed through me. I don't know whether my words were in a language he understood or whether God answered my prayer by speaking to the child directly and changing his fear to faith. I guess the explanation is immaterial. Whatever it was, it was a beautiful example of the supernatural power of a supernatural God who loves little Indian boys.

A year later I was back in South America, this time in Peru. The Wycliffe Bible Translators base in Peru is at a place called Yarinacocha, east of the towering Andes on the Ucayali River which joins the Maranon to form the Amazon River. The base is a mission compound, a sort of self-contained village in the heart of the dense Amazon jungle. Here the translators return from their remote Indian villages to work on the actual pen-to-paper translations.

The translators often bring several Indians out of the jungle with them to help with the translation work. These Indians prefer to live in small huts similar to those they have in the village, rather than in the larger homes occupied by the linguists and support personnel on the base. However, they are well accepted as part of the community.

One afternoon while I was taking a siesta in my small room on the river's edge, I had a visitor. Jim Daggett, an American linguist working with the Chayahuita tribe, was at the door. He had a concerned look on his face. It seemed his Indian helper, whom he had brought out of the jungle, a twenty-four-year-old tribesman named Miguel, was dying. He had not eaten in many days, and was too weak to stand up. Dr. Doug Swanson, the base medical doctor, had examined him. Although he could not find anything physically wrong, he confirmed his condition was *muy grave*. Miguel was begging to be returned to his parents in the tribe so he could die at home. However, before they took him back Jim wanted me to come pray for him.

"What do you think is wrong?" I asked.

"He's possessed with demons," Jim said soberly.

I had heard stories of Indians in the jungle who had even been killed by evil spirits, but had never had a firsthand encounter. On several occasions, back in the States, I had ministered to people who were under demonic influence, but never to anyone who was literally dying.

Jim went on to explain that when Miguel became a Christian the year before, the witch doctor put a curse on him. He told Miguel he would die unless he renounced Christ. Now, it seemed, the curse was coming to pass. Whether it was simply the power of suggestion or an actual demon who was strangling the life out of him was immaterial—Miguel was dying.

I felt totally inadequate. Yet how could I refuse this gentle request from this highly trained linguist who was giving his life to help these Indians. I agreed to go, although my faith was more than weak—it was nonexistent.

That evening several of us, including Jim and Dr. Swanson, went to Miguel's little hut. We found him, a handsome, brown-skinned man, lying on a thatched mat under a mosquito net. He was so weak he could not even open his eyes.

Dr. Swanson pointed out several vivid purple welts on Miguel's stomach.

"Suck marks," he said softly. "After the witch doctor cursed him, Miguel went to a second witch doctor and asked him to remove the curse by sucking. Those marks are blood blisters under the skin. They have been there six months."

I felt my hands grow clammy. "Why doesn't one of you pray for him?" I asked. "You know him better than I."

"We have," Jim confessed.

"But we're new in the Spirit. We thought maybe you . . ."

"But I can't speak his language," I objected. "He won't understand what I am saying."

Dr. Swanson put his hand on my shoulder. "We're not asking you to pray *to* him," he said kindly. "We want you to pray *for* him, using your prayer language."

I recalled many of my prayers for Americans back in the States. I would first analyze their situation, then tell God what needed to be done. "Lord, my brother has deep-seated problems. I ask you to heal that resentment he has toward his wife which came in when his mother spanked him at the age of three." Or, "Lord, his lungs aren't functioning correctly. You know how hard he's tried to give up smoking. God, give him new strength to stop, and while you're at it, Lord, he has a problem of biting his fingernails. You know how nervous he is because he lost his job and his son is smoking pot. . . ."

How foolish all that now sounded in the light of this situation.

Apprehensively, I knelt beside Miguel's corpse-like form and pulled back the mosquito net. The little hut was quiet with only the jungle sounds filtering through the thatch: the chatter of the monkeys, the squawking of the parrots, and the hum of a billion insects.

I swallowed hard. I knew, as a child of God, I had the same authority that Jesus had to cast out evil spirits. But it seemed so strange since the one I was praying for didn't know what was happening.

Then it dawned on me. He didn't need to know. I was not going to speak to him, but to the demons.

"In the name of Jesus Christ," I commanded, "I order you evil spirits to depart from Miguel and be cast into the middle of the sea. I bind you there forever."

I looked up. Miguel hadn't moved. His eyes were still closed, his face expressionless. I felt stupid. If only he could understand me. I could tell him to renounce the witch doctor. I could advise him to claim his deliverance. I could tell him that sometimes evil spirits come out by vomiting or coughing or screaming. . . . But none of my psychological manipulations were operative here in the jungle. I could preach all I wanted, to no avail. Miguel just lay there. Inert. Seemingly lifeless. However, I had gone too far to back down. I reached out and put my hand on his chest.

"Father," I prayed, "please send your Holy Spirit to heal all the wounds caused by the demons, and prevent them from ever returning again."

Then, suddenly, I was praying in my prayer language, using words only God could understand. Yet even as the Spirit prayed through me I was secretly hoping Miguel would understand the words, much like the little Indian boy in Colombia. But my "tongue" was obviously not in the Chayahuita dialect. If it was, Jim would have understood. No, this battle was being fought on a far different level from the mind—it was in the Spirit.

I looked up again. Nothing. Miguel still had not moved. But I noticed something. From the corner of each eye a tear had appeared and was running down the side of his bronze face, making a tiny streak in the dust.

"Amazing," Jim whispered reverently. Then, seeing my puzzled look, he continued. "These Indians never cry. Something is happening."

Two tears. That was all I had to rest my faith on. We replaced the mosquito net and left the hut. Miguel was still motionless on the rattan mat. I returned to my room feeling confused, almost defeated.

I was busy with my final interviews during the next several days and did not have time to go back and check on Miguel. In fact, I was afraid to ask about him and tried to put him out of my mind. From now on I would confine my prayers to people who understood English.

But the afternoon I was preparing to return to the States, Jim Daggett came by my room. I was just closing my suitcase.

"I wanted to tell you about Miguel before you left," he grinned. "The day after you prayed for him he got up and said he was hungry. I fixed him a big bowl of fish and rice and he ate enough to fill a horse. The next day he told me he wanted to stay here at the base and help with the translation."

I was amazed. "Did he understand what we did the other night?" I asked. Maybe, I thought, he understood my prayer language after all.

"No, I had to tell him about it," Jim confessed. "But now he plans to call all the other Indians together to tell them what happened. He wants them to know that in Christ they have more authority than the witch doctor, that they no longer have to live in fear of demons, but in the name of Jesus can cast them out."

Before I left that evening I walked over to Miguel's hut. He was healthy and smiling. There was something else. I noticed the purple suck marks on his stomach were almost gone. He had been healed—from the inside out.

How thickheaded I had been, trying to comprehend how this could happen unless there had been some kind of mental communication. It was difficult, but gradually I was beginning to understand: praying in the Spirit is the key that unlocks the door of the closet behind the place of the intellect, allowing the Holy Spirit to come into that deep level and bring to pass that which the conscious mind would reject if it tried to comprehend. One of the most important keys to inner healing is praying in the Spirit.

5

HANDLING YOUR AUGHTS AND ANYS

Nothing in the Christian life is more difficult, or more necessary for inner healing and spiritual wholeness, than forgiving those who have offended you or sinned against you. It was more than three years after I experienced the baptism in the Holy Spirit, though, before I began learning how necessary forgiveness is.

As a child, the summer week I dreaded most was the week our church set apart for Vacation Bible School. Not only was it an infringement on my vacation time, but I disliked being made a spectacle of when we were forced to march down the aisle of the church behind the flags singing "God Bless America." I hated having to make things out of pipe cleaners, saying a pledge of allegiance to the Bible, and gluing popsicle sticks together to make a hotpad for my mother.

I carried that same dislike for VBS into my ministry. Especially did I dread the opening day parade. The idea was to gather at the church early in the morning and decorate the cars with toilet paper and big poster signs that said, "COME TO VBS." The local fire department would send a truck and the cars, filled with screaming kids and driven by the women of the church, would line up to drive slowly through the sub-divisions—honking their horns and shouting at the children who ran into their yards to check the commotion. The pastor was usually the only man present (except for the firemen on the truck) and was expected to lead the parade, right behind the big, red fire engine. All summer long I would try to forget what was to come, but as the time drew near I would begin to have stomach cramps. By the time of the parade I would be praying desperately for a flat tire.

As our church began to break loose from some of the old traditions, we dropped a lot of these programs. However, primarily because of our strong-willed Vacation Bible School superintendent, Inez Thompson, we continued to have VBS. Inez had cut her teeth on VBS back in Texas and Oklahoma. Even though she was a close personal friend—and a deeply spiritual person—she refused to listen when I suggested we should omit it from the church program that summer.

"Call off the Sunday school if you please," she said stubbornly, "even stop taking the offering and put a bucket at the door. But we're going to have Vacation Bible School if I have to do all the work myself."

Inez was a hard worker. Dedicated to the Lord, she had been with the growing church from the first day we opened the doors. But I found her stubbornness irritating, especially her insistence that I take part in the school.

"Every year you plan your schedule so you are out of town during Bible school," she said in the early spring. "This year we're planning the school for the last of summer. I want you to promise me you'll be present. We need you."

70

I agreed, reluctantly. I arranged my calendar, making sure I would be in town that week. I owed it to Inez—and to the children.

We had a productive summer. I had accepted a job as a roving editor for *Guideposts* magazine and was enjoying the extra challenge of writing magazine articles, plus the close contact with some very dear friends on the magazine staff. The church was growing, moving more deeply into the life of the Holy Spirit. I was looking forward to the time when I no longer had to receive a salary from the church, but could support myself through my writing—pastoring the church as an avocation rather than a vocation.

As the summer drew to a close, Inez approached me weekly, reminding me of my commitment to be present for the VBS. Not only did she want me to lead the opening parade, but I was scheduled to lead a Bible study each morning at the joint worship service.

Then, on the Saturday night before the Bible school was to begin the following Monday—it was the second week of August 1971—I received a long distance phone call from my friend John Sherrill. John was at that time the senior editor of *Guideposts* and the man who was most responsible for my entrance into the field of professional writing.

John's usually cheerful voice was serious. He was asking me to join a small group of friends of Len LeSourd, who was the executive editor of *Guideposts,* and his wife, Catherine Marshall LeSourd, for a prayer retreat on Cape Cod. The infant child of Peter John Marshall, Catherine's son, and his wife Edith had serious congenital defects. The doctors said there was no hope for three-week-old Amy Catherine, but John felt that a few of us who were close to the family should gather around them in prayer during this critical time. Fifteen others were flying in from all over the United States. John realized it was

71

short notice, but asked if I could catch a plane the next day and join them, beginning Sunday night.

I knew I was supposed to go. Jackie agreed, but immediately reminded me of my promise to be present during the Vacation Bible School.

"Inez will have your head on a platter," she said. "You need to call her tonight and let her know."

But I was too cowardly. As long as I could remember I had been intimidated by authoritative women. No, I would rather face her the next morning at church and then slip out and catch the afternoon plane to Boston. It would be easier that way than trying to make an explanation over the phone.

The next morning the first person I saw as I came through the door of the Tabernacle was Inez Thompson. She immediately suspected something. "Don't tell me," she said half sarcastically. "You're leaving town during Bible school."

I swallowed. Hard. "I'm sorry, Inez. It's an emergency. I received a phone call last night and I have to fly to Boston. . . ."

She didn't let me finish. I saw the fire flashing in her eyes. "I knew it! I knew you'd find some way to weasel out of your responsibility! You never can be counted on for the really important things. You are constantly making promises and then backing down. Nobody can trust you! You're the most irresponsible person I've ever known!"

My cheeks were burning. I tried to interrupt and make an explanation, but she was in no mood to listen to my excuses. I finally turned and walked away, feeling her glaring at the back of my neck, which felt like it was on fire from embarrassment.

I wasn't very effective in the pulpit that morning. However, I had promised John I would inform the brethren in Melbourne of the situation. I knew they would want to join me in prayer for Peter John, Edith, Len and Catherine, and of course, little Amy. After I preached I asked if there were any present who would join me at the altar for a few moments of prayer before I left.

A number of people came forward and knelt with me at the altar rail. After most of them had returned to their seats, I felt someone kneel down beside me. Looking up, I saw Inez's tear-stained face.

"I'm sorry, Jamie," she said gently. "I was selfish in wanting you to stay when you are needed up there. Please forgive me for the way I acted."

I reached out and took her hand. We prayed together and I told her I understood. We embraced and then I had to leave. It was time to catch the plane.

Friends met me at Logan International Airport in Boston and drove me out to Peter John's little Community Church at East Dennis, on Cape Cod. The quaint white-sided church building was packed with people. They, too, were praying for the infant daughter of their young pastor. The evening service had already begun when we arrived and I was amazed to find Peter and Edith present in the service, along with most of the others from the special group. Instead of the somber atmosphere I expected, however, the group seemed filled with joy and victory. The service was one of great happiness as the people sang and praised God for His goodness.

I made my way through a side door and took the only seat available, in a side choir loft between Catherine Marshall and another dear friend, Virginia Lively. Like Catherine and myself, Virginia lives in Florida, and is well known among Episcopal circles for her ministry of counseling and healing. I slipped in between them, nodded to Peter who was leading the singing, and joined in the praise and worship.

It was almost heavenly. Never had I been in a service of such intense worship and joy. Even though little Amy Catherine was dying in Boston Children's Hospital, the people, including the parents and grandparents, were determined to praise God. I joined in, thanking Him I could be a part of such a time of worship among friends.

Then, suddenly, without warning, I began to feel dizzy. The more we sang and praised the Lord, the more nauseated I became. My head felt like it was caught in a giant vise and the pain behind my eyes was so intense I thought I was going to faint.

I turned to Virginia and said, with some difficulty. "Virginia, I've just become deathly sick. Please pray for me."

Virginia is a gracious, yet sometimes very blunt woman. A widow for a number of years, her time of walking with the Lord has given her deep insight into the things of the Spirit. She turned her head and looked deep into my eyes. "Jamie, is there someone in your life you haven't forgiven?"

That was all she said. She continued to stare for a moment and then turned back to rejoin the singing. I was aghast. I had asked for bread and it seemed she had given me a stone. I didn't want a sermon, I wanted prayer.

I started to object, but could say nothing. I closed my eyes and when I did, deep inside, in that secret place where God often makes me aware of His voice, I heard Him say:

"What about Inez?"

I wanted to argue with the Lord. I had forgiven her. I had even said so that morning at the altar rail. But the more I argued, the more I knew I hadn't. In fact, I had been sitting there thinking how good it was to be in Massachusetts sitting between Virginia and Catherine, rather than being back in Florida decorating my car with toilet paper.

The more I thought of this, the more I began to see Inez's side of the question. She had given months of her life to plan the Vacation Bible School. She wasn't doing it for herself, but for the children. And she was right in her accusations. I was an irresponsible louse. I had pulled this trick a dozen times in the past—not only with her, but with others as well. I was constantly making promises and then backing out in order to do something else which seemed more important.

And then, just as suddenly as the headache and nausea had appeared, it was gone. Vanished. I opened my eyes and realized I could sing again. I had been healed—not through the laying on of hands or prayer, but by forgiving that one against whom I had harbored resentment and by seeing the truth about myself.

The week went by in a hurry. The retreat was spent at the Community of Jesus near Orleans. We prayed for one another and prayed for the baby. Even though Amy Catherine eventually died, all of us who attended the prayer retreat knew that God had done a special work of grace in our hearts. Catherine, writing about that week in her book, *Something More,* said, "It was as if the tiny baby Amy became a divine catalyst, calling forth a concentration of God's power and love for others."

She was right. I returned to Florida chastened and eager to discover more about the healing power of forgiveness.

The very next week I locked myself in my little writing studio, along with my Bible and a concordance, determined to learn all I could about the Biblical concepts of forgiveness. If forgiving Inez, whom I loved, could bring instant healing, what power there must be if I went the extra mile and forgave those I didn't love.

The first verse I came upon was the one I had often heard David du Plessis use in his talks on forgiveness.

> *And when ye stand praying, forgive, if ye have aught against any: that your Father also which is in heaven may forgive you your trespasses (Mark 11:25).*

I sat for a long time looking at that verse. I slowly underlined it with my yellow felt marker. Surely this must be another of the keys to inner healing.

For some reason it never occurred to me that God's forgiveness of my sins (not His forgiveness of my Sin, for that was taken care of at Calvary and is an unmerited gift) was conditioned on my forgiveness of others. According to Jesus' statement, God would not forgive me as long as I held "aught" against anyone else. In my unforgiveness of others, I had blocked God's forgiveness for myself. No wonder I could get sick so suddenly. I had stepped out from under His protection.

I decided it was time to take stock of my relationships and see if there was anyone else I held aught against. Taking a note pad and pencil, I prayed, asking God to reveal anyone I had not forgiven. There was too much at stake—God's forgiveness of my own trespasses—not to do so.

As I prayed a man came to mind. It was the name of a young man who had been a part of our church in its early days when we were meeting in the lounge of an old hotel located on the Indian River in Melbourne. Steven was a young, energetic fellow with a small business and a large family. In 1967, just before Christmas, he had stopped by my home with a sad tale that he couldn't pay his rent, his children weren't going to have any Christmas, and his wife needed medicine. I believed him. After all, he was devoting as much time to the church as he was to his business—which was probably one of the reasons things were going so badly for him. I felt responsible to help, but when he told me it would take $400 to pull him out, I realized it was more than I had. Jackie was having to juggle our own checking account each week, trying to meet the needs of a young family with five children.

Still, we did have a savings account we had opened for the children. And since I knew Steven would pay me back, I dipped into it and withdrew $400—which was all the children had.

He insisted on signing a note with interest. "On or before May 1, 1968, I agree. . . ."

But long before May 1 rolled around, Steven and his

family had rolled out of town, taking up residence in a small town on the Gulf Coast of Florida.

I should have known better than to loan money to a friend. Give it maybe; but loan it, never. How well I remembered my dad quoting Shakespeare's advice in *Hamlet* when Polonius says to Laertes,

> Neither a borrower nor a lender be; for loan oft loses both itself and friend.

That's exactly what happened. A year later I wrote Steven a letter and sent it to his new address. "Forget the interest and just pay the principal," I wrote.

He wrote back. Business was bad, but he was due a bonus at the end of the year and would pay me off. In the future, he asked, would I send all correspondence to his office since matters like this upset his wife.

Another year went by and I heard nothing. "Matters like this also upset *your* wife," Jackie said. "I'm going to get some action." She picked up the phone and called his wife. She was extremely apologetic and a week later we got a check for $50 with a promise to pay the balance in monthly installments.

Two more years passed and we heard nothing. Gradually the situation began to eat away inside me. Sometimes at night I would lie awake thinking about how to get my money back, and my blood would boil. All kinds of thoughts came to my mind and once again I thought of Shakespeare. Only this time it was *The Merchant Of Venice,* as I identified with Shylock who, when he could not collect his debts, determined to collect a pound of flesh instead.

Now, sitting in my little studio with my Bible in my lap open to Mark 11:25, I realized that although the bad debt obviously wasn't affecting my friend, it had been tearing me all to pieces. Slowly I became aware of the spiritual damage it was doing as I stewed in my resentment and bitterness. Instead of feeling such seething reaction, I knew I should be praying for my nonpaying friend. But it was impossible. All I wanted to do was choke him until he spat up the money. And not only that, I found myself wanting to choke a lot of other people who had wronged me.

I returned to the Bible and the list of Scriptures on forgiveness. Before me was that familiar passage from the Lord's prayer:

> And forgive us our debts, as we forgive our debtors (Matthew 6:12).

I had repeated those words thousands of times, but had never seen them in this light. I actually had been asking God to forgive me the same way I was forgiving—or not forgiving—Steven. I trembled. What if God had answered that prayer? Surely He didn't lie awake at night figuring out ways to get even with me—at least I hoped not.

Every place I turned I found evidence of the truth that God was going to forgive me only in proportion as I forgave others. In one place Jesus said I was to forgive not seven times, but seventy times seven (Matthew 18:22). That added up to four-hundred and ninety times, and I couldn't even forgive once.

In another place He indicated even my gifts to God were unacceptable as long as I was unreconciled with my brother. That meant that although I had been tithing my income these last four years, I had missed the greater blessing from God because of my unforgiving attitude toward Steven.

"Oh, oh," I moaned, "the good news has become bad news."

But how could I forgive him? He owed me money and I still had the note to prove it. It didn't seem there could be true forgiveness until the debt was paid. It was then I discovered another verse which is surely one of the key verses to abundant living and inner healing.

> *And be ye kind one to another, tenderhearted, forgiving one another, even as God for Christ's sake hath forgiven you (Ephesians 4:32).*

I was to forgive Steven exactly the same way God had forgiven me—by paying the debt myself. Going to my file cabinet, I dug through the yellow manila folders and pulled out the four-year-old note. I wrote across the bottom, "Paid in full for Jesus Christ's sake. Ephesians 4:32." And I dropped it in the mail.

It was as though a heavy weight had lifted from my mind. Since Steven no longer owed me money, I could love him again—and my channel to love others was also unplugged. Returning from the post office, I could hardly wait to tell Jackie the good news. The debt was paid.

Jackie stood in the kitchen, stirring a big pot of vegetable soup, as I told her of my decision. Replacing the lid on the simmering cauldron, she turned and grinned.

"Great! When Steven gets that note it will really prick his conscience. I'll bet we have our money back in less than a week."

I reached out and pulled her close. Putting my finger on her nose in one of those little private affection touches which most husbands and wives develop across the years, I said gently "You don't understand. The note is paid. Now if he sends us the money, we'll have to send it back or give it away. It's not ours. He doesn't owe us anything."

Jackie nodded. "You mean like we can't repay God, because Jesus has already paid the price."

"Exactly!"

Interestingly enough, Steven did try to repay the loan. And

true to our commitment, we could not accept it. When he refused to take it back, saying it had weighed heavily on his conscience, we agreed to give it away. He did reluctantly accept our check when we returned the interest. The balance we sent to a Filipino pastor who is operating a struggling Bible school on the island of Mindanao. However, I am convinced the thing which set Steven free to pay the debt was my forgiveness. It was the perfect explanation of a verse of Scripture which had long been a mystery to me:

> *Verily I say unto you, whatsoever ye shall bind on earth shall be bound in heaven; and whatsoever ye shall loose on earth shall be loosed in heaven (Matthew 18:18).*

I had, in my spirit, bound Steven to the very conditions I wanted changed. By my unforgiveness I had stood between him and the Holy Spirit's work in convicting him of the debt he owed. By stepping out of the way through forgiveness, I had released him from judgment and opened him to hear from the Holy Spirit, and be convicted he should repay the money he owed. Not only that, but I had released myself to receive the forgiveness of God and step into a new dimension of abundant living.

Forgiving Steven was only the beginning. It was now painfully evident there were many other *anys* whom I held *aught* against. I needed to get busy.

The next one that came to mind was even more difficult, for I was sure the person had already died. In fact, he had been dead a long time and, besides, I didn't even know his name. Yet the aught had been swimming around in the lake of my subconscious for more than twenty years, causing untold problems.

In the spring of my senior year in college I bought a car to drive back to school. There were five of us, high school chums, who lived in the little town of Vero Beach, Florida, and had gone off to college together at Mercer University in Macon, Georgia. The other boys were as glad to see me get the car as I was. Now they could ride back and forth to school without having to spend all day and part of the night on a Greyhound bus. The car's maiden trip from Vero Beach to Macon came after the spring holidays. However, as we crossed the Georgia state line, I noticed the engine was running sluggish. I had filled the car with gasoline in Waycross, and by the time we got to Hawkinsville it was empty. I pulled into a little roadside garage and asked the mechanic if he could take a look at it.

He nodded and opened the hood. After a few minutes he withdrew his head and looked us over. It was obvious we were college kids, and of course the car had a Florida license tag. He pulled the stub of an unlit cigar from his mouth and wiped his greasy hands on a piece of red cloth which seemed dirtier than his hands.

"You boys just wander around town for a while," he said. "I think I can have this fixed in an hour or so."

An hour later we were back in the garage. He handed me a grimy piece of paper and said, "She needed a new carburetor. That old one was shot. You owe me thirty-five dollars."

Thirty-five dollars! That was all the money I had, and I expected it to last me until school was out. Still, my folks had warned me the car would be an expensive item and it certainly wouldn't work without a carburetor. I paid him in cash and we drove on north to Macon. It ran like a top and I concluded it was probably worth the money to get it fixed.

The next day I was showing off the car in the parking lot and asked one of my fraternity brothers, who had a reputation as a mechanic, to look at the engine.

"I just had a new carburetor put on," I said, "so I know that's in good shape."

After looking under the hood he said, "This isn't a new carburetor. It's the same one that's been on the car all along."

"But I paid that fellow thirty-five dollars for a new one."

My fraternity brother gave me a wide smile and said, "Old buddy, you bought yourself thirty-five dollars worth of screw adjustment."

I was furious. In fact, I was so angry I threatened to round up a carload of ATOs and drive back down to Hawkinsville and get my money back. I didn't, of course. I seldom do all the horrible things I threaten to do. But the resentment stayed with me, and from that time on, every time I drove through Hawkinsville I shook my fist at the old garage alongside the road.

A few years later, Jackie and I returned to Mercer for a visit. Driving through Hawkinsville I saw the old garage. Again the old feelings came bubbling to the surface. Anger. Bitterness. Hatred.

A number of years later we had to detour off the interstate highway and found ourselves once again in the small Georgia town of Hawkinsville. This time my children were in the car with us, and I deliberately drove down Highway 129 so I could point out the dingy old garage where I had been cheated. Inwardly I justified my actions, saying I needed to teach the children about dishonest mechanics who prey on unsuspecting people. What I was actually doing, however, was trying to get even by turning my children against my old enemy, the mechanic.

I didn't realize it at the time, but at that point I was treading on very thin ice. In reality I was usurping an authority that belongs only to God. God never allows His children the luxury of "getting even." In fact, He doesn't even allow us the pleasure of nursing hurt feelings. To do so is the basest sort of sin.

Dearly beloved, avenge not yourselves, but rather give place unto wrath: for it is written, 'Vengeance is mine, I will repay,' saith the Lord (Romans 12:19).

Inadvertently, I was committing the same sin that caused Lucifer, the anointed cherub of God, to be banned from heaven. In Isaiah 14 the prophet lists the seven "I Wills" of Satan (Lucifer) who determined to usurp the power and authority of God, setting himself above God's law, vowing to do the things that God had reserved for Himself. If God threw one of His servants out of heaven for such arrogance, what would He do to me? Yet in my unforgiveness I continued seeking vengeance, not realizing it was causing far more harm to me than to the one I hated.

The last time we came through Hawkinsville, the old garage was gone. It had burned down, or perhaps been torn down. All that remained was an empty field outside of town, covered with weeds, rusted auto parts, and decaying rubber tires. Yet as we passed the field there was still something inside me that raised its ugly head and cursed the old mechanic, who surely after all these years was dead and buried.

As this incident came to mind, I found myself raising the question: How can I forgive when the garage is gone and the owner dead? It was then the Lord showed me the secret of the *healing of memories*.

In the kingdom of God there is no time limitation. God, who lives in an entirely different dimension from us, is just as much a part of the past as He is of the present. I thought of the old Gospel song we used to sing:

When the trumpet of the Lord shall sound
And time shall be no more . . .

The Bible says Jesus Christ is the same yesterday, today, and forever. He is not a part of this earthly kingdom which is limited by calendars, watches, yesterdays, and tomorrows. It is just as easy for Jesus Christ to reach back into the past and bring forgiveness as it is for Him to touch us today, this instant.

Thus one afternoon, sitting in my car in a Melbourne, Florida gas station while the attendant checked under my hood, I determined it was time to take care of this old "aught." I let my mind flash back to that afternoon in Hawkinsville when the old mechanic, with grease under his fingernails and a cigar in his mouth, had cheated me. In my mind I relived the event, and as I did I saw something I had never seen before. The man was ignorant of his sin. Oh, he knew he was cheating me; it was a way of life for him. He felt no qualms about taking advantage of a car full of college kids. But then I saw him through the eyes of Jesus, and I was suddenly filled with an enormous love. So much love, in fact, that my eyes drowned in tears as I thought of all the hatred I had spewed out against him over the years.

"Oh, God," I said inwardly, "forgive me. I didn't know what I was doing either." And the task was done. I saw Jesus standing in the garage, watching the old man as he took my money. I saw him when the next car of college boys came through, and he cheated them also. Jesus had been there all along, saying to the Father, "He doesn't know what he's doing." Jesus was not condoning his sin, nor was He trying to hide it. He was just forgiving it the same way He forgave those men who drove the spikes through His hands.

There are some who suggest the way to healing of the memories is by pretending certain things didn't happen. But God is a God of truth. He says that in the end everything that is covered shall be uncovered. Healing does not come by pretending, nor by imagining things could have been different. It comes by looking at our fellow men through the eyes of Jesus—and forgiving as God, for Christ's sake, forgives us.

There were many other anys whom I held aught against. There was a woman in South Carolina who had lied about me. She had done it deliberately and it had caused deep hurt to my wife and my children. And would you believe I even discovered resentment against a little boy, a neighborhood bully, who had punched my son in the nose fourteen years before. I had quickly controlled my anger in that situation, but in reality I had not dealt with it for I had never forgiven the boy. All I had done was push the memory of the incident down beneath the surface of my conscious mind into the reservoir of my subconscious. When I began probing around, I quickly realized it was there. Still, unforgiven. I handled him, along with the woman from South Carolina, the same way I took care of the mechanic from Georgia. In each case I was so immersed in love that I found myself weeping in conviction as I saw them through the eyes of Jesus. I was experiencing what Paul was talking about when he said:

> *The love of God is shed abroad in our hearts by the Holy Ghost which is given unto us (Romans 5:5).*

But the biggest aught was yet to come. My father was an astute and honorable businessman. He had moved to Florida from Indiana at the close of World War I and become a pioneer in the citrus industry. The east coast of the state was virtually uninhabited in the early 1900s and he helped carve the niche where the little town of Vero Beach now rests. One of the advantages of pioneering is you get to pick up some excellent real estate. Besides the various citrus groves he owned or had an interest in, Daddy purchased forty-eight acres of choice property as his own personal homestead. He cleared part of the land and had it planted in select citrus. There was every imaginable type of fruit: oranges, grapefruit, tangelos, tangarines, kumquats, limes, and many varieties in between. Part of the sector was left in virgin foliage, called a "hammock" in Florida. Another part of it was fenced-in pasture to take care of the several cows and small herd of Shetland ponies which we raised and sold on the market. Although our pasture adjoined the municipal golf course, which one day would make it extremely valuable, our nearest neighbors were more than half a mile away. It was "country living" at its best.

The crowning glory of this beautiful piece of property was the house Daddy had built. Daddy never believed in borrowing money—for anything. His business acumen helped him save, however, and when he learned an entire boxcar of California redwood had been mistakenly sidetracked in Vero Beach and was for sale, he waited until the price was right and bought it to build his house.

What a house it was. Solid redwood. Two stories with sixteen big rooms. The floors were of hard oak and the formal staircase, extending up from the living room, was of birdseye cypress—polished to a gloss. Walls and ceilings of all the rooms were lightly stained in green, red, brown, or pale yellow to preserve the grain of the double-notched, tongue-and-groove six and eight-inch planks. The outside was redwood siding, painted to preserve it against the salty air which blew in from the nearby ocean. Inside the only place we saw paint was on the bathroom and kitchen ceilings. Everything else was wood, beautiful wood.

One of Daddy's greatest innovations was the raised bathtub in the big upstairs bathroom. There were five of us children, four boys and a baby girl, and Daddy knew the rigors of having to bend over a bathtub to scrub backs and then get rid of the pesky ring on the tub. So he instructed the carpenters to raise the big six-foot tub thirty inches off the floor. Underneath were drawers for towels and at the end was a set of steps, guarded by a handrail, for entering and departing.

The entire house was like that. An upstairs clothes chute emptied into a dirty-clothes closet downstairs near the kitchen, which was a fine place to romp and play (or to be locked in for disciplinary purposes). A huge attic added another floor to the house and provided a wonderful place to work on model airplanes, make toy soldiers from a hot lead smelter, or rummage through Daddy's old World War I relics.

The wooden walls and ceilings acted as sounding boards so that even though my two older brothers, Walter Jr. and Clay, were in a room down the hall from the room where my younger brother and I slept, we could still talk through the house after the noise of the day subsided.

In those night hours I loved to lie on my bed next to the open window and listen to the outside noises: the steady whirr of the crickets harmonized with the percussion sounds of the frogs. The melody was sung by the plaintive calls of the whippoorwills, and sometimes, when the nearby hammock was bathed in moonlight, the solo parts were carried by the great owls hooting as they answered each other back and forth through the woods.

It was on a night such as this, when I was thirteen years old, that I overheard a conversation between my mother and father. It was long past the time when everyone should have been asleep and the only sound in the house, other than the occasional creaking of the boards as they cooled off, was the echo of the deep tick-tock of the grandfather clock which hung on the landing of the stairs. For some reason I was still awake, dreaming those wonderful dreams of early adolescence which spring from a happy and secure childhood. I could tell by his steady breathing that my younger brother, John Ladd (we called him Laddie then, although now that he has picked up a string of impressive medical degrees he goes by his formal name of John), was asleep. Just as I was drifting in and out of slumber, I recognized my mother's voice coming through the slightly ajar door.

My older brother, Clay, was the apple of her eye. Five years my elder, he was a senior in high school and was by far the most popular boy in school. An all-state football and basketball athlete, he had just received a Congressional appointment to the

U.S. Military Academy at West Point. I almost idolized Clay, for he was all the things I wanted to be when I entered high school. Clean cut, disciplined in his studies as well as his athletics, deeply moral—it's no wonder my mother was so proud. He had given her his gold footballs and basketballs, awarded him for stellar athletic performances, and she had them made into a necklace which she wore with unabashed pride. I think it embarrassed Clay a little, but he loved and honored his parents. His mother could do no wrong—even when she was bragging on him.

That night I heard her talking softly to Daddy, who was in the other bed. Still basking in the glory of Clay's appointment to West Point, she said: "I'm so proud of Clay. He's the finest son we have."

There was more, but that was all I heard. Already sensitive over the inordinate attention my older brother was receiving from my mother, I closed my mind. It was as though she had said, "I love Clay more than I love Jamie." And suddenly, as though it was built with concrete blocks, there appeared a wall between me and my mother—a wall which was to remain for almost twenty-five years.

The disease of unforgiveness spread until it infected my relationship with all women—especially those who bore authority. Women were to be used, manipulated. The thought sometimes occurred to me that had not God put His hand on my life in such a dramatic way, I had the makings of a Lothario. Fortunately this was buried so deeply in my lake, and covered so thoroughly with the grace of God and the love of my family, that it never did come to the surface. But deep inside I knew there lurked an exaggerated awareness and declaration of masculinity—a macho attitude—which was determined to assert itself over all female figures.

My relationship with my mother seemed, on the surface, to be loving and healthy. When we did have clashes—as we usually did when we were together—we blamed it on "temperament" differences. Now I realize that temperament is nothing more than the exhibition of the subconscious. If the inner lake is filled with unforgiveness, then your temperament will reflect it. If the subconscious has been made transparent through forgiveness, then things will be much, much different.

However, even though I was able to camouflage my feelings about my mother, others—especially those closest to me—noticed them. Jackie, in particular, recognized it. Often when I would flare up at her, she would quickly analyze the situation and say, "I remind you of your mother, don't I?"

She was right. Especially was this true when she tried to assert herself against my will. In the deep places of my mind I had long ago disqualified my mother's right to assert herself in my life. In my thinking, if she didn't love me, then she had no right to tell me what to do. Across the years, as this lie got buried deeper and deeper in my lake, it finally took on the shape of "no woman has the right to tell me what to do." It was for this reason that Inez Thompson, and a host of other strong-willed women, caused me to react with hostility—even though I thought I loved them deeply.

Yet, strangely, on the other hand, I was putty in the hands of a woman who was tender, gentle, and submissive. I recognized this, and in the midst of some of the raging arguments which often erupted between Jackie and me, I would abruptly stop and say, "Just love me, Honey. Don't shout at me, just come and hold me and I'll be all right."

Recognizing that my personality suffered from a kind of spiritual malnutrition caused by the shut doors of unforgiveness, Jackie learned that I could be brought into a semblance of emotional balance through a great deal of affectionate coddling. But we both knew this was sick. I was still a little boy demanding to be my mommy's favorite.

Thus, as I ran this deep inventory on my subconscious,

checking out the aughts and anys, I eventually got to that massive closed door—my relationship with my mother.

However, recognizing it existed only heightened the confusion. I knew I had to forgive her. But how? She was now in her mid-seventies, and over the years our relationship had improved to the extent that I loved her far more than I ever dreamed possible. In fact, not only did I love her, but I had grown to respect her judgment and appreciate her deep commitment to the Lord. She was by far my strongest supporter and biggest fan. If it were possible, I think she would have had the dust jackets of my books reduced to miniature form, gold-plated, and made into a necklace. How she delighted in bragging about me, loving my children, and showering her affection on Jackie. In fact, as I examined that door more closely, I saw it was only a shadow. Somewhere, across the years, it had disintegrated. Perhaps it happened when I received the baptism in the Holy Spirit, perhaps long before. Now all that remained was an image. Yet that image was just as real as if the solid door were still there, for it had kept her out of the inner place of my life, and kept me from reaching out to her in genuine love and trust. My mother wasn't the problem, I was.

"Let me show you something about those kinds of doors," God seemed to say to me one morning when I was praying. "None of them are real. Once a door like that is bathed in the blood of my Son, Jesus, it disintegrates. True, it may look as if it is still there. But it's there only in your imagination. I have set you free."

I was reminded of the experience of Simon Peter in Herod's prison. Arrested following the execution of the Apostle James, he was chained in a prison dungeon between two soldiers who kept constant watch over him. Between him and freedom were three massive gates and sixteen soldiers charged by the king to guard him specifically. Yet that night an angel of the Lord appeared in the cell, opening the doors, loosening the chains, and causing a deep sleep to fall on the guards. Even so, Peter was not free until he got up from the dungeon and walked through the open doors and out into the city (Acts 12:1-19).

I realized I would never be free from the specter of that dark night when I imagined my mother no longer loved me, until I walked through the door of forgiveness—a door already opened by the work of Jesus in my life.

"But how do I do it, Lord?" I asked. "Surely you don't expect me to go to my mother, after all these years, and say, 'Mom, I forgive you for leaving the impression you loved Clay more than you loved me. It's caused me years of heartache and problems, but I forgive you for Jesus' sake.' Surely, Lord, you don't want me to say anything like that. That would be cruel."

"You're right," the Lord said quietly. "Besides, most of those problems were of your own doing. All I want you to do is look at your mother the way I look at her, and love her the way I love her."

"I do love her," I answered.

Then it was I discovered how to tell a person you forgive them. You do it by telling them you love them. Genuine forgiveness will always manifest itself in love. In fact, if it doesn't cause you to love the person forgiven, there is good reason to doubt the sincerity and genuineness of your forgiveness. You love because you forgive. Forgiveness is an act of the will. Love is the result. The fact that I really loved my mother was evidence that I had already, sometime in the distant past, forgiven her. There was nothing more that needed to be done—except express that love through action and word.

The way to say, "I forgive you," is to say, "I love you."

Several years ago I attended a three-day retreat at the Methodist Youth Camp near Leesburg, Florida. Even though the retreat was scheduled during an extremely busy time of my life, I welcomed the opportunity to withdraw with members of our church family and spend a relaxing time in fellowship and prayer.

Shortly after we arrived at the beautiful camp which is situated on Lake Griffin, one of those sparkling lakes which dot central Florida, I began to feel uneasy. As that first day wore on I gradually became aware that my uneasiness was in some way connected to the fact that the camp was owned and operated by the Methodist church. In fact, just seeing the signs on the buildings, and walking into the chapel and seeing the Methodist hymnals in the pew racks, gave arousal to feelings of bitterness. Why, though, should this make me feel uncomfortable? After all, some of my earliest childhood memories were related to the Methodist church where Daddy taught Sunday school.

That evening, as I sat in the back of the chapel listening to one of my friends lead the Bible study, it slowly dawned on me that I still held aught against the Methodist church back in Vero Beach. During my high school years I attended, along with many of the members of the football team, Sunday evening activities at the local Methodist church. We enjoyed the fun and food served by the Methodist Youth Fellowship (MYF) and especially was I drawn to the personable young pastor who often joined the football team during afternoon workouts. He was a "swell guy," in the vernacular of the high school athletes. He came to football practice dressed in sweat clothes, ran wind sprints with us, and acted as the unofficial chaplain for the team. Coaches and players alike appreciated his presence.

But his relationship with the boys never went any deeper than that. When one of the boys on the team got one of the cheerleaders pregnant, he went to the pastor—only to be referred to a social worker in the community. The boy later told me that he really wanted an experience with God, he wanted to be forgiven for his sins, but the pastor seemingly missed that point altogether.

One night after MYF the pastor asked me if I would speak

during a youth night service. I was thrilled and scared. But later, when I went to him for help, the best he could do was give me a book of devotions and suggest I memorize one of them for my talk. At the last minute I called him and told him I didn't think I could speak. He laughed and said I was a terror on the football field, but a chicken in church. I agreed, and we left it that way. Gradually I dropped out of the Methodist church and drifted across town to the Baptist church where my girl friend attended.

However, across the years I began to blame much of my lack of spiritual understanding on that Methodist pastor. He had an ideal opportunity to turn a whole football team towards God, but rather than run the risk of losing some by getting too spiritual, he had opted to cling to his role as a "swell guy."

Somehow I transferred his failure to reach me to the church he represented, the Methodist church. In my mind it was really a denomination which had failed me, not just a minister. Working on this premise I began to see many other flaws in the Methodist church. When some of my friends said their literature no longer honored Christ, I agreed. When a renegade Methodist pastor accused the church of turning from the heritage of John and Charles Wesley to a social Gospel orientation, it gave additional fuel to my fire. For years this thing had smoldered deep in the back of my mind, sending up dense clouds of smoke which prevented me from ever seeing any good in the entire Methodist denomination. Now, closeted away for three days in a Methodist camp, all these memories came floating to the surface. I knew they had to be dealt with. But how?

The last morning at the retreat I rose early. Tiptoeing out of my cabin in the gray of the dawn, I wandered down a wooded path to a secluded spot beside the lake. There, under giant overhanging oaks, I found a seat on a cypress stump in a spot designated "the chapel in the woods." Chin in hands, I sat brooding, wishing I could forgive and clean my mind, but not knowing how. After all, the literature *was* socially oriented, and there was a lack of emphasis on spiritual things. How could I forgive when the very things I held as aughts seemed to be true?

As the sky turned from gray to rose and the first rays of the sun reflected off the rippling waters of the lake, I became aware of a life-sized cross which had been erected near the water's edge. At least the Methodists still held to the "form" of Christianity, I conceded.

For a long time I sat, looking. The only sounds were the noises of nature—the twittering birds, the lapping water, the swish-swish of the limbs in the trees. I couldn't get my eyes off that cross, silhouetted against the rising sun. What would it be like to touch it? To place my arms against the outstretched beams? No one in the camp was yet stirring. If I was ever going to do an odd thing like that, now was the time.

I don't know how long I stood there, arms outstretched, hands pressed against those rough, splintering beams. Gradually, though, I began to tire. My shoulders ached and my arms were weary. But I would not take them down. I wanted to stay on forever, where my Lord had hung.

I felt my arms falling and reached for the top of the crossbeams to hold on. Each second seemed meaningful. But as I gripped the tops of the crossbars, I noticed something strange. The texture of the wood was different. On the sides it was rough, rugged. On top it was smooth.

Painfully, I realized what it meant. I was not the first to put myself against that cross. Countless others—those Methodists whom I had criticized as "un-godly" and "un-spiritual"—had been there before me. By the hundreds. Perhaps thousands. It was their tired hands which had worn the wood smooth.

I returned to camp, chastened. That morning in the Bible study in the chapel, as we sang from the Methodist Hymn Book, the words took on a new meaning. I saw things from a different perspective. By the time we left that afternoon to drive back to the east coast, my whole manner of thinking had changed. In a final time of devotions, before we broke camp, I led the group in a prayer of thanksgiving for our Methodist brethren who had built that camp for the glory of God.

Everything, I discovered, looks different when you view it from the cross. It's there that inner healing begins—and finds its fulfillment.

6

MY WORLD UNDER WATER

It was a strange group, the sixteen of us who gathered that quiet August morning in 1971 in the big, sunny living room of the Bethany retreat house of The Community of Jesus on Cape Cod. Some of the people I knew, some I had only heard of through Len and Catherine LeSourd. We were all there for a common purpose, to surround Catherine's son, Peter John, and his wife Edith with our love—and to pray for tiny Amy Catherine who was in the Boston Children's Hospital, ninety miles away, slowly dying.

None of us knew how long we were supposed to stay, nor had any plans been made other than we were to eat our meals in the big community house where we were meeting. There was no leader, although we were looking to John Sherrill, who had made the arrangements for us to stay at the Community, and to Len who, although very soft spoken and easy going, was by nature a leader. The Community of Jesus is made up of several

97

houses situated on the edge of Cape Cod Bay at Rock Harbor, a little fishing village near Orleans. In some vague way it resembled a Protestant monastery composed of both single girls who committed themselves to chastity and service, and families which maintained their own homes in the immediate vicinity and were deeply submitted to one another and the Community leadership. We were simply using their facilities.

After breakfast that Monday morning we gathered in the big living room with its large windows facing the undulating waters of the bay. Seated in a rough circle around the room, we listened while Len suggested we take turns introducing ourselves and stating any personal needs. I welcomed this approach, for it would give me an opportunity to meet those I was seeing for the first time. On the other hand, it seemed a bit strange to begin this way, since we had gathered primarily to pray for the baby.

Each one of us took a few minutes to state where we were spiritually. Several in the group were exactingly honest and talked about their need for inner healing. All seemed to believe God had called us together so we could be cleansed in the deep areas of our lives.

About mid-morning we took a break and enjoyed tea and cookies served by one of the "sisters" of the Community—a beautiful young woman dressed in a simple blue and white uniform who padded in silently with a tray of goodies, smiled, and disappeared back into the kitchen. A few moments later we rejoined the circle and listened as Peter John gave us the latest report on Amy Catherine. Several in the group expressed a desire to drive into Boston and lay hands on the baby, praying for her healing. Others were more cautious, feeling we should do nothing until we had direct "guidance" from God. We agreed to wait, pray, and do only that which had the approval of the entire group. Already, in those few short moments, we had taken on the aspect of a church: a group of called-out ones, committed to the lordship of Jesus Christ and submitted to one another. We sat silently, waiting . . . praying.

Outside I could hear the Indian summer wind blowing in off the bay and moaning around the eves of the big house. The brown and tan sea oats, which adorned the sand dunes between the house and the water, moved gracefully in the wind. A brilliant red cardinal pecked at the sill of the large picture window, sharpening his beak on the stone. I glanced around the room and felt that strong familiar surge of love for each one present. I closed my eyes and blended my mind with theirs, and with God, seeking His guidance for that hour.

Something was happening. A firm impression was forming in my mind concerning the woman sitting across the room in a wingback chair. I had met her for the first time only that morning. She was the wife of a well-known American businessman who could not come to the retreat, but had urged his wife to take his place. I knew, from her brief introductory statement as we shared earlier in the morning, that this kind of retreat was a new experience for her. Yet I had the strongest feeling she was to be a vital part of what God was doing this week. Since we had agreed to share any impressions of guidance with the entire group, I spoke out.

"I feel a small group is to drive into Boston and lay hands on Amy Catherine. I also have the strongest impression that you—and I pointed my finger at the woman and called her name—are to go along and hold the baby while the others pray for her."

I heard a gasp from across the room. The woman's face blanched. "How can you say that? You don't even know me." She was obviously frightened. This concept of sitting quietly and hearing from God was strange and unfamiliar to her. She looked across the room at Catherine, who was the only person in the room she knew well, and said, "I can't do a thing like that. All the rest of you people are Christians. I don't even know what is going on here. I'm just here because my husband sent me. I'm not worthy to hold that baby. I don't even know how to pray. . . ." She was weeping by this time and suddenly every mind in that room focused away from that tiny baby in the Boston hospital, and centered on this other child, sitting in our midst, who was also dying—not physically, but of a far worse spiritual malady.

Catherine got up from the sofa where she had been sitting beside Len, crossed the room, and knelt down beside the woman's chair. In just a few moments, using passages of Scripture which had been familiar to her since childhood, Catherine led her to the place of committing her life to Jesus Christ. The rest of us in the room watched, in delight, as the gloom and fear on her face gave way to joy, much as the darkness of night is dispelled by the coming of the dawn. She looked around the room as though she were seeing us for the first time—her eyes brimming with tears of happiness.

Charles Hotchkiss, a young Episcopal priest from Florida and a long-time friend of the LeSourds, left his chair and stood behind her. I sensed what was about to happen. Gently he laid his hands on her head and began to pray softly. The rest of us in the circle joined hands, forming a ring of prayer around Father Hotchkiss and the one for whom he was praying. She was slowly lifting her hands above her head and then out of her mouth, softly at first, but plainly audible, came unintelligible sounds, a heavenly language. Gentle and beautiful, the sounds flowed from her lips like the trickling of spring water over smooth rocks. Her eyes were closed and her face was bathed in a soft glow, the light of peace. I bowed my head and held back the tears, tears that always seem to come when I am in the presence of one so gently touched by the Holy Spirit. For a moment I sensed what it must have been like, those many years ago, when Simon Peter came to the house of Cornelius and this identical thing happened. Yet this wasn't the Book of Acts, nor was it the city of Caesarea—it was the twentieth century and we were on Cape Cod.

Nothing had been said about "praying in the Spirit." No one had coached her. To my knowledge this was her first experience in any kind of group where something like this might occur, yet none of us had indicated we used a prayer language. It had come directly from God.

As the ecstasy subsided, the rest of us moved in to embrace her, then to embrace one another. The room seemed saturated with love and joy. Then John Sherrill, in a cheerful voice, made a staggering question.

"Why don't we go all the way? We have witnessed conversion and the baptism in the Spirit. Why don't we have a water baptism service as well. After all, we have access to the biggest baptistry in New England, Cape Cod Bay. Surely it's deep enough for her to be immersed."

It was a fabulous idea—at least to a confirmed Baptist like myself—but I was astonished that it came from John, whom I knew as a rather traditional Episcopalian.

John gave me an "oh-I-thought-you-knew" laugh and proceeded to tell me that he and his wife, Elizabeth, had recently been immersed in Charles Hotchkiss's Episcopal church in the little Florida town of Clewiston.

It was no wonder the group was excited over the prospect of another water baptism service. Peter John and Edith both injected that they, too, had been praying about water baptism and felt this was their time also. We agreed to hurry and change clothes, for the tide was beginning to ebb in the bay. If we didn't get to the water quickly, all we would find would be miles and miles of exposed mud flats until the tide returned.

I had a kind of inner excitement about the matter. I knew I was the only Baptist in the group and even though Father Hotchkiss had immersed a few people recently, his experience at conducting water baptism services was nothing compared to mine. It seemed natural that I should "officiate" at the service, a position which seemed very important to me because of my personal insecurity about being among these giants. These others might be experts in their fields—writing, editing, or the healing ministry—but I was an expert baptizer.

But God had other ideas and as the group left the house to make our way over the sand dunes and through the waist-high sea oats toward the water, I suddenly found myself in His presence. It was one of those rare times when I knew the Holy Spirit was teaching me. It developed into a dialogue as we headed toward the bay.

"You're not going to do the baptizing," He said. The voice, although not audible, was just as real as if I had been standing in a classroom talking to a teacher.

"But I'm the most qualified. Besides, I want to. I *need* to." I had so little I could hold out as trophies to make others notice me. Surely God would recognize my experience and not take this one claim to fame away from me. After all, it would be quite a feather in my hat to say I had officiated at this historic baptismal service. How blind I was to the deeper things of the Spirit. How desperately my inner man needed healing.

"No, I am not going to let you do the baptizing, because your own water baptism was out of order."

I knew, of course, what He was talking about. It had bothered me, on and off across the years, but like a lot of other things which were not quite right, I had stuffed it down beneath the surface of my lake and tried to forget about it. It was only on occasions like this, when the Holy Spirit stirred the waters, that the question ever surfaced.

During my teenage years I had joined the First Baptist Church of Vero Beach, Florida. A lot of kids joined the church during adolescence, and the fact that the girl I later married was already a member was all the incentive I needed. In order to become a full member of the church, I needed to be immersed. I talked to the pastor and then on a Sunday morning, prodded by my mother who also felt it was proper that I join a church, I walked down the aisle and was received with what Baptists called "the right hand of fellowship." A week later, on a Sunday night, the pastor ushered me into the church baptistry and, suitably adorned in a white robe, I was immersed.

But there had been no accompanying spiritual experience, no surrender of my will to Jesus Christ's. Even though the words were used, they were simply words. It wasn't for several years, when I found myself at that campfire service on an island in Schroon Lake, New York, that I made the necessary spiritual commitment to the lordship of Christ.

Across the years I knew my water baptism had been "out of order." I had known this, and at times it had bothered me. However, after a number of years in the ministry, my pride became strong enough to keep those troublesome thoughts from rippling the surface very often. After all, what would people think, if after all those years of baptizing other people, I admitted I needed to be baptized? Wouldn't they lose confidence in me if I let my mask down and confessed this spiritual tangle in my life? No, it had seemed best to simply leave it alone. No one really cared when I was baptized and as long as there were no questions, why should I stir the waters and cause confusion.

But God is never finished with a man until he is conformed to the image of His Son. In this case I knew the matter of water baptism was second in importance to the fact I had been living a lie all those years—and was satisfied with it. Some matters can be handled by confession and absolution. In other matters confession is not enough, a person needs to set things right. My water baptism was one of those things that I could no longer push beneath the surface of my lake and pretend all was well. It was time to make the correction. Publicly.

"But who will perform those baptisms if I don't?" I asked the Holy Spirit.

103

"Why, Charles Hotchkiss, who else?" He responded.

I dreaded asking the next question for I already knew the answer. "And who will baptize me?"

"Charles Hotchkiss," the Spirit answered—and I could almost hear Him chuckle. "You'll be the first candidate when we get to the bay."

"Oh, God!" I moaned inwardly. "He's an Episcopal priest and I'm a Southern Baptist minister."

This time it seemed the Holy Spirit laughed out loud.

However, in my obedience to the command of God, something else happened. In fact, it happened even before we reached the water. When the Holy Spirit decides to teach a lesson, He can do it in split seconds. In my case, He did it as I was gingerly making my way through the sea oats, making sure my bare feet did not step on something sharp.

Immediately I began to think of the sins I had served—the elements in life which had controlled me. For years I had been a slave to strawberry shortcake. While others might have been addicted to alcohol or drugs, I was addicted to food. In short, I was a glutton. I was also fat. Not "stocky," but blubbery fat. I carried around my waist more than twenty-five pounds of excess flesh. I had been on every diet imaginable, but all they did was set the stage for a subsequent weight gain.

I had taken up jogging, but a huge brown dog with blood-shot eyes and claws that went "clickety-click" on the concrete behind me sent me into wind sprints for home.

"Your brother, who is five years older than you, does one hundred push-ups each morning," my mother bragged. Having competed with Clay all my life, I decided to get the Royal Canadian Air Force list of calisthenics and start to work. It was hopeless. There never was any time, and when I finally got around to it, my teenage daughters went into hysterics. "Daddy, it shakes like jelly!"

I had resigned myself to remaining fat; yet deep inside I knew I wasn't supposed to be that way. One of my positive-thinking colleagues said the answer was to "think slim." But it's hard to think slim when you have difficulty bending over to tie your shoes. One clothing store clerk even had the audacity to say, "Sir, if you'll stop holding your breath, I can get a correct measurement." No amount of thinking slim would take care of my problem. It was far deeper than that, stemming from an inner condition of insecurity and bondage which caused me to crave food even when I wasn't hungry.

Now I began to realize that water baptism was another key to inner healing, for in submitting I was actually appropriating the death of Christ to my own subconscious appetites:

> *That like as Christ was raised up from the dead by the glory of the Father, even so we also should walk in newness of life (Romans 6:4).*

Suddenly I was filled with a new excitement that this could be one of the turning points of my life; that in water baptism I was actually going to leave my old worldly appetites under the water of Cape Cod Bay—which, symbolically, was ebbing out to sea and taking all the old pollution with it.

We arrived at the water's edge and I pulled Father Hotchkiss aside, asking if he would grant my unusual request and baptize me first, even before the now-excited woman who, only moments before, had accepted Christ as Lord. (By the way, she later accompanied a small group of us to the children's hospital in Boston and did hold Amy Catherine while we prayed for her. And even though the child died just two weeks later, I understood that this new change in the woman's life, coupled with her willingness to hold that tiny baby while we prayed, brought about a marvelous new relationship with her own daughter—a relationship which had been strained for many years.)

Father Hotchkiss asked me a few questions, for he was as mystified over my request as I. However, he agreed to take me into the water first. He quickly made it plain that if I was to submit to water baptism, I would also have to submit to his method.

I had no sooner agreed than he turned to the group which had assembled on the beach and said, "Jamie wants to go first, but before I baptize him he wants to confess his sins before you."

I hadn't counted on that. But I had come this far and there was no use in stopping. If my friends rejected me on the basis of my sins, that was their problem, not mine. I was determined to go all the way and leave my world under water.

So I named them: gluttony, lust, resentment, unforgiveness, pride, self-righteousness . . . on and on the list went. It was difficult, and terribly embarrassing. If there was any group in the world I wanted to impress with my spirituality, this was it. Yet I knew God was pleased.

We waded out into the bay which by that time was visibly receding. I crossed my hands in front of my chest, waiting for Father Hotchkiss to lower me backwards beneath the water.

"On your knees!" the priest said.

I started to protest, but I remembered I had agreed to do it his way, no matter how strange it was. I dropped to my knees on the sandy bottom. The warm water came up to my chest. I felt the priest's hand on the back of my head and realized I was getting ready to go under face first. As he offered a brief prayer, I looked down into the ebbing water of the bay and repeated that prayer of commitment which Jesus prayed on the cross, "Father, into thy hands I commend my spirit."

I came up, shaking the water out of my ears, just in time to hear the priest say, "That's for the Father." Then, before I could catch a good breath, I was under again. This time for the

Son, and finally, a third time, for the Holy Spirit. I guess he figured he'd never get his hands on another Baptist minister.

Something did happen out there in the water, something in my inner spirit which had to do with discipline. I had begun a fast that day which I expected would last three days—which was the longest I had ever been without food. Instead, it lasted twenty-eight days. During that time I began to experience a new surge of spiritual authority. Not only were my old "appetites" being broken, but by the time I returned home at the end of the week, I felt like Moses descending from Mt. Sinai with the tablets of stone in his hand and the radiance of God on his face. Apart from my experience with the baptism in the Holy Spirit, nothing had so visibly shaken and shaped my life as did my submission to water baptism. It was, in fact, another step to the healing of the inner man.

Almost at once, however, I realized that testing always accompanies fasting. It was the same with Moses. After forty days of fasting and communing with God, he returned from Mt. Sinai only to find the children of Israel had gone wild—rebelling against God, practicing licentiousness, and worshipping a golden idol which had been fashioned by Moses' brother Aaron. Something akin to this happened following Jesus' water baptism at the hands of John the Baptist. He was led by the Spirit into the wilderness where he fasted.

> *And when he had fasted forty days and forty nights, he was afterward an hungred. And when the tempter came to him, he said, If thou be the Son of God, command that these stones be made bread (Matthew 4:2, 3).*

It seems there is a biblical principle here. Every mountain top experience is followed by a valley. But it is in the valley that the true temper of the steel is tested. It is only when a life is under pressure that a person can determine if there are leaks.

107

Several years ago we installed an underground sprinkling system in our yard. With the help of my children, I finally managed to dig up the yard and lay what seemed to be endless miles of plastic pipe. Then, using an abundance of tape, glue, and clamps, we got the thing hooked up. Like repairing a locomotive that is underway, the job was technically interesting, but not much fun.

A friend gave me a rebuilt three-quarter-horsepower pump which I hooked to a pipe that ran into the lake behind our house. Presto, we had water on the lawn.

But something was wrong. The water was not evenly distributed, and unless we had a strong east wind, a portion of the yard never got wet. The little pump simply did not have enough power to give pressure to all those sprinkler heads. I had a choice of blocking off most of the sprinklers or getting a more powerful pump. I opted for the pump.

After three months of fiddling with the system, I finally went out and bought a brand new three-horsepower pump. The salesman assured me it was big enough to water the lawn of the White House. I spent most of a Monday running a larger intake pipe out into the lake and installing the new self-priming pump. Then came the moment of truth as I stepped inside the back door and flipped the switch. The pump whirred into life and we had water. I mean we really had water!

Where my old system—held together with glue, rotting tape, and rusty clamps—had been sufficient for the three-quarter-horsepower pump, it was totally inadequate for this new big pump which exerted more than four times the amount of pressure. Water squirted everywhere. Underground connections burst loose and erupted in the yard like geysers, blowing dirt and grass up with them. Tape peeled off exposed connections, sending out streams of water. Tiny pinholes in the pipes, unnoticed before, suddenly opened and sprayed water in all directions. Loose sprinkler heads exploded off their connections as the water roared upward in gushers higher than the roof of the house. Flaws, blemishes, and defects which had remained unnoticed were suddenly exposed as the new power surged through.

So it was when I came off my twenty-eight-day fast. All my spirituality was gone—in the testing time after that fast it just gushed out of my inadequate piping system. I found myself with a ravenous appetite and was constantly losing my temper over the most inconsequential things.

"If that's what being baptized in water does to a person," Jackie commented one evening after I had just lost my temper and slammed a door, "then you better not recommend it to anyone else."

I was chagrined. Yet even so I knew that something had happened to me. It was not just an emotional kick, I had literally moved into another dimension of life. Despite the fact there was still much evidence of the old life, I suspected it was something like a snake shedding its skin. The old skin was still there, and quite obviously a part of the snake, but it was dead. And in due time it would come off and be left behind. For the first time in my life I began to look at my defects and flaws not as insurmountable problems, but as challenges to be conquered—and left behind.

Someone said, "I don't care how loud you shout, or how high you jump, as long as you walk straight when you hit the ground." I was beginning to understand that. It's not the start, it's the finish that counts; and until I allow the Holy Spirit to take total control of *all* my life, I will still have to go through the times of testing. If it was true for Jesus, how much more so for me.

Paul told the Ephesians to be strong and *stand* against the trickery of the devil. In fact, he used the word "stand" four times in that strong passage of Ephesians 6:

> *Put on the whole armour of God, that ye may be able
> to stand against the wiles of the devil . . . wherefore
> take unto you the whole armour of God, that ye may be able
> to withstand in the evil day, and having done all, to stand.
> Stand therefore (Ephesians 6:11, 13, 14).*

There comes a point, he was saying, in your Christian
experience when God has done for you all He can do. He gave
you His Son. He gave you His Spirit. He gave you His Word.
He emptied Heaven and gave it to you. There is nothing more
God can do. It is at this time that God asks you to stand.

There are some situations that can be changed directly by
prayer. There are other situations that can best be changed by
personal counsel. Conversely, there are some situations that can
be changed by healing or deliverance, but there are other situations in which God requires a person to *stand*. That is why Paul
said four times: "Stand therefore . . ." (The Greek word
means to stand as a conqueror.)

There is a teaching going out through the Church that you
can praise your way out of anything. I believe in praise. It is a
great and wonderful and powerful tool. But it can be a very
injurious thing to teach people all they have to do is praise, no
matter what is going on, and they'll come out of every situation
bouncing and springing. It is more complicated than that.

The same is true with any mechanical device of religion:
water baptism, healing of the memories, deliverance, even
prayer. There will come a time in your spiritual life, if you walk
deep enough with the Lord, when you will eventually run into
the principalities and powers. At this time, when you are involved in spiritual warfare that is so deep and complicated that
you can't even describe your feelings with accuracy, there is but
one thing you can do. Stand.

One of my favorite Bible stories centers on Moses at the

Red Sea. The Egyptian armies were closing in on the Hebrew people who were fleeing from Pharaoh across the desert when ahead of them loomed the Red Sea. There was no place to go. The enemy was behind them and the sea before them. The people, frantic with fear and anger, turned on Moses, their leader.

> *Were there no graves in Egypt, hast thou taken us away to die in the wilderness? . . . It had been better for us to serve the Egyptians, than that we should die in the wilderness (Exodus 14:11, 12).*

Moses' answer to their bitter clamoring must certainly be ranked as one of the great passages of all history. Turning to the people he said calmly,

> *Fear ye not, stand still and see the salvation of the Lord, which he will show to you today. . . . The Lord shall fight for you, and ye shall hold your peace (Exodus 14:13, 14).*

In so many words he was saying what Paul later advised the church at Ephesus: *Don't just do something, stand there*.

My own personal test came shortly after I returned from Cape Cod and the fast was finally over. During the four years following my baptism in the Holy Spirit, our Baptist church in Melbourne, Florida, had made rapid strides toward taking on the shape of a New Testament body of believers. However, the closer we moved to New Testament forms and patterns, the further we were removed from our denominational traditions—and the more we seemed to agitate the other Baptist churches in our local association. The week I ended my fast I was called before the Executive Committee of the Brevard Baptist Association to explain our actions in dissolving our

111

membership rolls in favor of an open membership.

I tried to remind these other Baptist pastors that Baptists had always believed in a New Testament structure for the local church. We were just trying to put that into effect, and since I could find no authority in the Bible for having a church membership—or for that matter, dividing ourselves into separate denominations in order to exclude other Christians from our fellowship—we were simply transcending the man-made traditions to return to the patterns of the Book of Acts.

The pastors were kind, but firm. They wanted us out of the Association. I suspected the real reason lay in the fact that many of the people in our rapidly growing congregation spoke in tongues and we often had public healing services. However, this was never mentioned since Baptists also believe strongly in the autonomy of the local church and these men knew if they began a doctrinal investigation of our church, they would open themselves to a similar investigation themselves. None of them wanted that.

So, on the basis of a technicality—the fact that the Associational Constitution and By-laws said that only ''members'' of a local Baptist church could attend the associational meetings— they voted unanimously (I abstained from voting) not to seat any messengers from our church if they showed up at the annual associational meeting the following week.

I was crushed. Their action was tantamount to casting us out of the Southern Baptist Convention, since membership in the SBC was contingent upon membership in the local association of churches. My roots ran deeply into the Baptist heritage. I had attended a Baptist college and held degrees from a Baptist seminary. For fifteen years I had pastored Baptist churches. I had served on various committees and boards on both state and nationwide levels. My parents had donated the old homestead, those forty-eight acres of choice land in Vero Beach, Florida, as well as the beautiful old redwood house, to the state Baptist convention to be used as the Florida Baptist retirement center for aged Baptist ministers and laymen. Now we were being thrown out, and the only reason given was we had departed from the Baptist tradition.

My old nature said I should make a fight of it. I knew we were on scriptural ground and felt if our people attended the annual associational meeting the next week, en masse, that we could probably prove our point and rescind the action of the Executive Committee. Even if the vote went against us, our action would surely cause enough commotion to get us space in both national news coverage and in the various state Baptist papers.

I called a meeting of the deacons of our church and their wives and told them of the action of the associational Executive Committee. Still riding the spiritual "high" of my water baptism and lengthy fast, I naively assumed they would side with me. Instead I discovered several of them felt the same as the Hebrews at the Red Sea. "Why have you brought us this far? We never did want to leave Egypt in the first place. We've been Baptists all our lives and even if you say there is some kind of Promised Land out there, we don't want to have to walk through the wilderness to get there. Why did we ever have to get into all this free worship and association with Presbyterians, Methodists, Catholics, and Pentecostals? It's all your fault."

I was angry. I had followed God and I expected them to follow me. Instead I found that even though they were camping in Goshen, their hearts were still in Egypt.

However, four of the families, the ones I most suspected would have wanted to remain in the Baptist fold, took another slant. Inez and Woody Thompson, their daughter and son-in-law, Allen and Saundra Reed, Allen and Carilyn Aden, and another dyed-in-the-wool Baptist family, Brooks and Laura Watson, pulled me aside after the meeting and gave me some surprisingly sage counsel.

"Any time you start off through virgin territory," Brooks said, "you're going to run into obstacles. God has brought us this far; we can't turn back now."

The others agreed. They had as much to lose as I, but were determined, now we had done all, to stand.

We agreed together that we had more important things to do than fight our brethren. By common consent we decided not to send any representatives to the annual associational meeting. We would lie down and die without a struggle. God would fight our battles for us.

Like my water baptism experience in which I died to self, this turned out to be one of the greatest things to happen in the life of our church. Within a year our attendance doubled—and the offerings tripled. People were driving from miles around to attend the services because they knew that regardless of their former or present church affiliation, they would be welcome in this body where the only thing that held the people together was the love of God—not a doctrinal statement, a denominational charter, or even a membership roll.

None of us have regretted that we let God fight that battle for us. Inner healing, we discovered, could be just as meaningful on the corporate level as it was on the individual level. In this case, an entire church decided to take up the cross and die with Jesus. The results were the same as take place when an individual is buried with Him in baptism—you rise to walk in newness of life.

7

DELIVER ME FROM EVIL

No study of inner healing or spiritual maturity is complete without a chapter on deliverance from evil spirits. Unfortunately, most studies on inner healing look upon deliverance the same way a physician might view a peddler of snake oil elixir, while books on deliverance have a tendency to lump all personality problems under the heading of "demon possession."

I have no illusions that, in this short chapter, I do the subject justice. However, there are certain areas of our lives which cannot be handled through the regular channels of prayer, forgiveness and commitment. These are areas of demon control and harassment and they must be met head on, in the name and under the authority of Jesus Christ. In short, demons are not prayed away, they are cast out.

I doubt if I would have included this chapter in the book had it not been for a conversation I had in Germany soon after I finished the rest of the manuscript. Jackie and I were staying with a United States Army chaplain in Wurzburg during a four day teaching conference sponsored by the ·Wurzburg Chapel. One evening, after we had returned from the conference, we were sitting in the chaplain's comfortable living room, sipping coffee and giving him a chance to catch up on news from the States. He asked me about a mutual friend.

When I mentioned things had not gone too well with him he put down his coffee and said, "Oh, in what way?"

I dislike being the carrier of bad news. In this case, however, since we were talking about a common friend, and since our motives were prayerful concern and not idle gossip, I felt free to mention a few things. His deteriorating family situation, his bad health and, just recently, my concern for his emotional and spiritual state.

The chaplain sat back in his chair and closed his eyes.

"Do you know . . . ?" and he mentioned the name of another minister.

I nodded, wondering why he brought up a second name when we hadn't closed the first subject.

"Is it true that he, too, got into the same problems as our other friend?"

I was concerned. I had known this chaplain for a number of years, and this kind of muckraking was out of character. However, I nodded my head. "That's what I understand," I replied.

He called another name, a teacher I knew of. "I understand she has just written a book," he said.

"That's right," I answered, still puzzled over this line of questioning.

"Have you read it?" the chaplain asked.

Something strange was going on, but I couldn't quite fit it together. "Yes," I replied. "But there were some things that bothered me—ideas which bordered on the metaphysical and psychic. I'm afraid she is actually being led into deception."

The chaplain named two more well-known ministers. One of them had fallen into severe moral disorder and the other, sadly, was teaching an obvious false doctrine.

"You're leading up to something, aren't you?" I asked.

He nodded his head seriously. "All five of these people have been close friends of mine. Several years ago, when I was a junior grade officer at a military post in the east, we were all involved in a search for deeper spiritual truth. During their search, however, they became involved in the occult, attended seances and even used Ouija boards. Later they all received the Holy Spirit. Now, however . . ." and he dropped his head before continuing, "one by one they are turning from the truth. Deceived."

"I don't understand," I said honestly.

He then reminded me of something which I, myself, had once written for Corrie ten Boom. It was Tante Corrie's story of closing the circle. I sat back, remembering how Corrie, in her Dutch accent, had first told me her story of "Closing the Circle."

It would seem, after having been a Christian for almost eighty years, that I would no longer do ugly things that need forgiving. Yet I am constantly doing things to others that cause me to have to go back and ask their forgiveness. Sometimes these are things I actually do— other times they are simply attitudes I let creep in which break the circle of God's perfect love.

I first learned the secret of closing the circle from my nephew, Peter van Woerden, who was spending the weekend with me in our apartment in Baarn, Holland.

"Do you remember that boy, Jan, that we prayed for?" Peter asked.

I well remembered Jan. We had prayed for him many times. He had a horrible demon of darkness in his life and although we had fasted and prayed and cast out the demon

117

in the name of the Lord Jesus Christ, the darkness always returned.

Peter continued, "I know God had brought this boy to me not only so he could be delivered, but to teach me some lessons, too."

I looked at Peter. "What could that boy, Jan, so filled with darkness, teach you?"

"I did not learn the lesson from Jan," Peter smiled. "But from God. Once in my intercession time for Jan the Lord told me to open my Bible to I John 1:7-9. I read that passage about confessing our sin and asked the Lord what that had to do with the darkness in Jan's life."

Peter got up and walked across the room, holding his open Bible in his hand. "God taught me that if a Christian walks in the light then the blood of Jesus Christ cleanses him from all sin, making his life a closed circle and protecting him from all outside dark powers. But—" he turned and emphatically jabbed his finger into the pages of the Bible—"if there is unconfessed sin in that life, the circle has an opening in it—a gap—and this allows the dark powers to come back in."

Ah, I thought, *Peter has really learned a truth from the Lord.*

"Tante Corrie," Peter continued, "even though I was able to cast out the demon in Jan's life, it always crept back in through the opening in the circle—the opening of Jan's unconfessed sin. But when I led Jan to confess this sin, then the circle was closed and the dark powers could no longer return."

That same week the wife of a good friend came to me for counseling. After I had fixed her a cup of tea she began to tell me about all the people who had prayed for her, yet she was still experiencing horrible dreams at night.

I interrupted her conversation and drew a circle on a

piece of paper. "Mary," I said, "do you have unconfessed sin in your life? Is this the reason the circle is still open?"

Mary said nothing, sitting with her head down, her hands tightly clasped in her lap, her feet together. I could see there was a strong battle going on in her life—a battle between spiritual forces.

"Do you really want to be free?" I urged.

"Oh yes," she said.

Suddenly she began telling me about a strong hatred she had for her mother. Everyone thought she loved her mother, but inside there were things that caused her actually to want to kill her. Yet, even as she spoke, I saw freedom coming into her eyes.

She finished her confession and then quickly asked Jesus to forgive her and cleanse her with His blood. I looked into her eyes and commanded the demon of hatred to leave in the name of Jesus.

What joy! What freedom!

Mary raised her hands in victory and began to praise the Lord, thanking Him for the liberation and forgiveness He had given her. Then she reached over and embraced me in a hug so tight I thought she would crack my ribs.

"Dear Lord," she prayed, "I thank you for closing the circle with your blood."

(*Logos Journal,* Mar/Apr 1974, pg. 11)

Tante Corrie's principle was easily applicable to the situation described by the chaplain. Because the five people had been involved in the occult, the door of deception apparently was still open, a door which could only be closed through confession and repentance.

There is much discussion these days as to whether or not a Christian can "have a demon." One of my friends says a Christian can have anything he wants. But that's too simple. Perhaps it's more accurate to say that Satan has no claim on that part of the soul which has been crucified with Christ. But if there is a part of the inner man—the soul—which we deliberately refuse to surrender to the Lord, then that part of us is still open to receive demon spirits.

In a fine explanation of this matter Frank Longino, Jr., a pastor/teacher in Louisville, Kentucky, writes:

. . . Recoiling from a word like possession, many have concluded that Christians are not invaded in any serious way by demons, they are just harassed from the outside. Doing away with the word, possession, we can then say that anyone, including Christians, can come under demon control in some area of his life. If it is just beginning, he can probably handle his own deliverance by taking authority over it. If it is a severe measure of control, he may need to be "delivered" by someone with this ministry.

In the Scripture, demons are always cast *out of* persons, not "off" them. In all of this, it is extremely important to know where one has left the door open to these spirits so as to be able to close it. Open doors are usually places where we are knowingly disobedient to God, or they may be unworthy habits and attitudes that we refuse to let God deal with in our lives. . . .

Disobedience to God's law for our lives is always dangerous. For a Christian to knowingly live in disobedience to God is to open the door wide to demonic control in that area of disobedience. Some Christians have a quick temper and do nothing to curb it, or to allow God to deal with it. This opens the door to demonic control. Some allow resentments to develop into bitterness and outright hatred until these attitudes and spirits are beyond personal control. This is demonic control. Some persons are controlled by habits of various kinds. A habit that is not dealt with could become an open invitation for demonic control.

Paul says, "I will not be brought under the power (authority) of any" (I Corinthians 6:12b). . . .
(*Logos Journal,* Jan./Feb. 1974, pg. 19)

Frank's insight helped me understand a situation which
arose in our church several years ago.

Elaine Randall was a 49-year old, slightly graying wife of a
retired military man. Childless, she and her husband were active
in the church and eager to make a contribution to the kingdom.
One Sunday night, after church, she stopped me on the sidewalk
and asked if I had any typing she could do. I was, at that time,
behind on a book manuscript. She was elated over the chance to
help and insisted on doing it without pay. She stopped by the
house early the next morning to pick up the first five chapters
which were ready for final typing.

A week later I dropped by the Randall's small home in a
quiet subdivision. Elaine's husband, Harry, was working in the
yard. He waved and pointed toward the back door.

"Go on in. She's working in the den."

Elaine glanced over her shoulder as I came in. "You're
just in time," she said with a cheery smile. "I'm just finishing
the last page now. I don't know when I've had so much fun."

I stood in the doorway, watching her peck away at her little
electric portable. I hadn't noticed it before, but Elaine's fingers
were stiff and swollen with arthritis. I watched as she struck the
keys and could tell they were sensitive. She was in obvious
pain, yet she continued to type.

I have suspected, for a long time, that arthritis has its roots
in unconfessed resentment and bitterness. I let the thought run
through my mind. Should I broach the subject with Elaine? Yet,
she was giving me so much, should I not give her the benefit of
this spiritual knowledge. I was naive enough to think that
everyone was as excited about deliverance and healing as I was.
I hesitated, but as Elaine pulled the final sheet of paper from the
machine, I asked the question.

"How long have you had the arthritis?"

She carefully stacked the paper with the rest of the manuscript and for a moment, I thought she had not heard my question. But she sat motionless, staring down at her brittle fingers which were now resting in her lap. I walked over and laid my hand on her shoulder.

"Elaine, I don't believe God intends for you to suffer with arthritis. Have you ever wanted to be free?"

"A million times," she said softly, still looking down at her crippled hands.

"Could there be areas in your life, in your childhood even, where you still nurse resentment—areas where you've been hurt or wounded and the root of bitterness is still there? Arthritis is often the result of this kind of experience."

I felt her stiffen under my hand. She turned and glared. "I don't believe that," she spit out. "And even if it is so, what business is it of yours?"

Almost as if I had thrown a switch, her personality changed. Her eyes narrowed. Her lips were white and quivering. "If you don't like my typing just say so. After all, I'm not getting paid, you know."

It was a ruse. She was trying to throw me off, trying to set up a roadblock so I would detour. I almost took her bait, tempted to try to defend myself. Then I realized what was happening and once more I moved back in, knowing the authority of Christ in me was far stronger than the demonic force at work in her.

"There *is* something, isn't there. Some deep hurt. Some . . ."

I didn't have a chance to finish. She dropped her face into her hands and began to weep, convulsively. She finally looked up. Her mascara had run down her face and one eyelash was askew. "I can't talk about it now. Give me some time."

I took her hand, wet with tears, and prayed with her. She

tried to apologize but I picked up the finished pages and started out. "The battle's ninety per cent won," I grinned. "I'll be back."

She nodded and squeezed my hand. "I do need help," she said softly. "Thanks."

It was just one month later when the opportunity arose. Elaine had finished the manuscript, and though she refused to accept any payment, she and Harry did agree to let Jackie and me take them to dinner. We chose a quiet little seafood place overlooking the Indian River and spent an enjoyable evening in the nearly empty restaurant, savoring a delicious meal. After we had finished, as we sat drinking coffee, I started probing again.

"Let's talk about your arthritis," I said, looking at Elaine across the table. "And about your past."

For just an instant I saw that same evil spirit start to exhibit himself. But she had promised, and by an act of her own will she kept it under control. She glanced over at Harry, who nodded, and then looked back at me.

Gradually the story unfolded. Her mother had died when Elaine was four years old. Her father had disappeared soon after, leaving her to be raised by her mother's mother. The grandmother was bitter, and filled with hate toward the deserted father. She lost no time in passing it along to Elaine.

"She used to come into my room at night," Elaine said softly," after I had gone to bed, and tell me bedtime stories about my father. She told me how worthless he was. He never could hold a job. She said he was responsible for mother's death and then he ran away. He didn't love me. He didn't love anybody. She said he was as mean as Hitler."

This hate, planted by a grandmother, was so real and deep in Elaine's life that even as she talked her teeth clenched.

In most cases, hate is an attitude brought about by unforgiveness. But in this case I realized the hate ran far deeper than unforgiveness, and remembering the hostile reaction of a month before, I suspected demonic activity. Elaine's grandmother had caused her to hate someone she couldn't even remember, and hate him so badly it was now destroying her body.

Forgiveness was not enough. In fact, years later, Elaine had set out to discover the facts about her real father. She couldn't believe he was as wicked as her grandmother had said. She learned her father had died. But she also discovered that he was actually a kind, tenderhearted man who had not been able to find work during the depression. When his wife died he had an emotional breakdown. Broken in heart and body, he left his little daughter in the hands of the only person he thought could care for her—his wife's mother. The father had spent time in a sanitarium, had become an alcoholic, and before he died wrote a letter telling his daughter, whom he hadn't seen in twenty-two years, that he loved her more than anyone on earth.

Yet, knowing all these facts, Elaine was still unable to love him. The demon, planted in her soul by the vengeful grandmother, caused her to hate her father with a fury.

I paid the check for the dinner and the four of us walked out on a small dock behind the restaurant which extended into the river. The spot was deserted and we sat on a weathered wooden bench, watching the black ripples on the surface of the water reflect the silver of the almost full moon.

"Do you think I have a demon?" Elaine asked softly.

"That's not the question," I answered. "The question is, are you sometimes controlled by a demon—and does your arthritis have its root in the bitterness toward your father?"

"Will you minister to me?" she asked sincerely, her voice shaking. "I want to be set free."

"I'm not the one to do it," I said, gently touching her elbow. "Tonight, after you get home, I want you to submit to Harry's ministry. Let your husband be the one to take authority over this spirit."

It was about noon, the next day, when I heard from them

124

again. Harry came by the house so excited he could hardly talk.

"I've never seen anything like it," he said. "The minute I began to tell the demon to leave she turned on me. She told me we were all crazy, that the two of us were conspiring against her, that I was just as evil as her father. . . ."

Harry glanced at Jackie who was standing in the door, listening. "I know this sounds ridiculous, but I grabbed her and shouted at the demon to come out in the name of Jesus. She screamed so loud I thought she would wake the neighborhood, and then just collapsed in my arms, weeping. Then she began naming other spirits which she said had come into her life. She renounced jealousy, envy, a spirit of control, a dominating spirit . . . we were up until almost three o'clock. But when we went to sleep there was peace in the house."

Once the root of bitterness was plucked out and she was set free from the bondage of hate, she could deal with the other attitudes which had so long warped and twisted her personality. This kind of recognition and repentance is absolutely necessary in order to receive inner healing.

Three weeks later I stopped by Elaine's house to take her some revisions on the book. She met me at the door, held out her hands and said simply, "Look!"

The arthritis was gone. Her fingers were slender and straight. She laughed as she clasped and unclasped her hands.

"I don't know when it disappeared," she said. "But when I sat down at the typewriter yesterday to write a letter, I noticed the swelling was gone." Then she began to cry, only this time her tears were mingled with sounds of laughter and praise.

I wish there was a happy ending to this story, but instead it almost parallels the story Jesus told of the man who swept his house clean but refused to fill it with the Holy Spirit.

When the unclean spirit is gone out of a man, he walketh through dry places, seeking rest, and findeth

none. Then he saith I will return into my house from
whence I came out; and when he is come, he findeth it
empty, swept and garnished. Then goeth he, and taketh
with himself seven other spirits more wicked than himself,
and they enter in and dwell there: and the last state of that
man is worse than the first" (Matthew 12:43-45).

During the next year, as our church moved into a free
worship, I noticed Elaine resisting. I could see it in her face on
Sunday morning. Harry was open, and seemed to enjoy the new
freedom, occasionally raising his hands and singing the new
choruses. But Elaine disliked the change, and gradually I saw
the old bitterness and arrogance beginning to return.

One Sunday morning I was standing on the platform as the
congregation began to sing a new, lively Scripture chorus.
Elaine stiffened as the piano picked up a bouncy beat and the
people began to clap in time to the music. Directly behind her
was a tall, heavily bearded young man. He was singing loudly,
and clapping his hands. Elaine's face was like a frozen mask.
She turned slowly and gave the young man an icy stare. Fortunately, his eyes were closed and his face upturned in worship.
But when Elaine turned back, I saw the old demon of hatred had
returned.

Across the months it became worse. I tried to talk with her,
but she refused to listen. Harry just shook his head, sadly. "All
she talks about," he said, "are those strange people who are
taking over *our* church." Then he added, "And it's beginning
to bother me, too."

I realized the Randalls' spirit was affecting me, and, as a
result, affecting the entire congregation. If the congregation
began to sing some of the new choruses I would glance at Elaine
to see how she was faring. If her face was screwed into a tight
mask (as it usually was) I was tempted to quench the Spirit in
order to keep her happy. Gradually it dawned on me that the evil

spirit, now operating in the Randalls, was holding back the entire spiritual progress of the church.

Jackie and I went by their house to talk. Harry was not there, but we sat and talked seriously with Elaine. "We love you deeply," I said. "But we know you are unhappy with the way things are going."

"Who's unhappy," she snapped. Then she added with vengeful sarcasm, "Don't you remember. I was delivered of all that?"

"We want your love and friendship," Jackie said gently. "But we also want you to be free. Even free to leave the church if you wish."

"Now you're trying to get rid of me," she snorted, her face contorted in hate. "Well, we know when we're not welcome. . . ."

We stayed a while longer, trying to work things out. But there was no way. Harry came in just as we were leaving and I put my arms around him. He stiffened, and I knew that he, too, was now infected. Deliverance was available, we knew that from the past, but unless a person wants to be set free. . . .

The following week the Randalls were not in the service. A month later we received word, through a friend, they would not be back. Ever.

It was almost three years before I saw them again. I had stopped by the hardware store one Saturday morning to buy some new sprinkler heads for my infamous underground sprinkling system. As I was coming out I almost bumped into Harry, who was picking up a small bag of fertilizer from the sidewalk display. He was his old, affectionate self and I was suddenly effused with love for him.

"How's Elaine?"

"Oh, she's out in the car. Come speak to her."

I leaned through the window to kiss her cheek, but she pulled back. She was talking through a mask, but beyond the facade I saw the demon spirit, still glaring back through her eyes.

We chatted for a moment and I started to leave. But as I did I glanced down at her hands. Her knuckles were badly swollen, much worse than before, and her fingers were bent and twisted from the arthritis.

I waded in. "How are your hands, Elaine?"

For just a moment I saw her true self trying to break free. Her face went tender and in her eyes I saw instant tears. She knew what I was offering, and she wanted to reach out.

Then, like a cloud slipping over the sun, the evil spirit drew the blinds and her eyes went dark.

"Let's go, Harry," she said. "You wanted to get that stuff on the grass before it rains. Nice to see you Jamie. Tell Jackie hello." And they were gone.

I wanted to hold them back, but in this case there could be no deliverance unless there was a desire. I had to let them go, but my heart still, to this day, aches with sadness when I think of what they had, and refused to keep.

Elaine had not closed the circle. Satan and his demons had been evicted from land they formerly occupied, but then, in a deliberate act of defiance, Elaine had once again stamped Satan's passport with a valid visa and given him entrance into her life. Only through confession could she cancel the visa—but her pride was too formidable a barrier to allow that to happen. She was trapped in a prison of her own making, tormented by a demon to whom she had issued a personal invitation.

The Bible has a great deal to say about a worldwide kingdom of darkness in which Satan is king and the fallen angels rule under him as princes over countries, cities and people. By their control over men they control both the world systems and in some cases, even the organized church.

Demons are under the lordship of Satan and he uses them to

oppress, vex, afflict and torment men. They are named, often, by the results they produce in the lives of men.

Some demons that are named in the Scripture include:
a blind and dumb demon (Matthew 12:22)
a dumb and deaf spirit (Mark 9:25)
a spirit of infirmity (Luke 13:11)
unclean spirits (Acts 5:16)
seducing spirits (I Timothy 4:1)
a spirit of divination (Acts 16:16)

These demons can come in through a variety of entrances. One of the most common is occult practices. The rise of eastern and oriental religions—all of which are demon oriented—has opened the door for a new wave of demonic oppression in the United States. These include not only the Jeanne Dixon, Edgar Cayce concepts, which are merely underworld practices dressed as angels of light, but the practice of many things considered by the general public as harmless fads. A partial list of such practices, all of which open the mind for entrance of demons, would include:

Ouija boards
palmistry
handwriting analysis
automatic handwriting
hypnotism
incantations
charms
necromancy
transcendental meditation
hari krishna
yoga
extrasensory perception
gazing

astrology
levitation
fortune telling
water witching
tarot cards
witchcraft
black magic
white magic
seances
spirit guides
scientology
crystal ball gazing
clairvoyance

Hypnotism may not necessarily be evil within itself, but it

is certainly a door through which evil spirits may enter. It demands the submission of the will to another person in a manner that belongs to God alone.

One of the saddest stories in my experience surrounds the former pastor in my community. Soon after I received the baptism in the Holy Spirit he contacted me to let me know he was in great sympathy with my new direction. In fact, he said, he had found a similar source of power in "ethical hypnotism." He went on to describe how a young man in his church, through a posthypnotic suggestion given him by the pastor, had been "delivered" of fingernail biting. I was ignorant of the dangers of this type of thing back then, but something deep in my spirit warned me to stay clear. In less than a year the pastor had resigned and moved to Colorado to teach in a large institution majoring on hypnotism. The last I heard of him he had left his wife and children and moved to California where he was roaming the beaches as a fifty-year old hippie.

Much of what we call "harmless" is poison in a jar with a medicinal label.

Strange as it may seem, another avenue through which demons may enter is music. In fact, music is often called the "language of the soul." The "soul" being that basic nature of mankind.

King Saul, when he was troubled by an evil spirit, was soothed by David's harp-playing, since David sang and played songs that were inspired by the Spirit of God.

Mother Basilea Schlink of the Evangelical Sisterhood of Mary in Darmstadt, West Germany, points out that in the final analysis, it is not the words of the songs that are decisive, but rather the spirit behind the music. Hence Scripture prefaces its words about singing and making music in the church with "be filled with the Holy Spirit" (Ephesians 5:18). Music written under the inspiration of the Holy Spirit remains, generation after generation, to bless and inspire. Handel's *Messiah*, written under divine anointing, is a good example. However, melodies which have been inspired by bad spirits, no matter how religious the words may seem, will not be able to impart a spiritual blessing.

One evening, when our oldest son, Bruce, was a senior in high school, he developed an excruciating pain in his ear. We were up with him most of the night, doing all the things we knew to do. We checked to make sure it wasn't a draft of cold air. We put hot compresses on his ears. And we prayed. We prayed a lot. But nothing seemed to ease the pain. By morning the pain had diminished and he was able to go off to school, although he was in poor shape from loss of sleep. That night, however, the pain reappeared, even more intense. The next day we took him to the doctor.

The doctor made a thorough examination and could find no evidence of infection, although his ears were red and inflamed. He told him to take aspirin, use some ear drops, and stay out of the water. That night the pain was even worse.

I went in and sat on the side of his bed, feeling helpless as I watched him clench his teeth and writhe on the bed. The only way he could find partial relief was to sit up in bed. So, we sat and talked, long into the night.

Finally, near midnight, Bruce said, "Dad, there's something I want to tell you. But I don't know how."

"Try me, Bruce, I don't shock easily," I smiled.

"About a week ago something came into my room," he said seriously. "It was early in the morning. I was just waking up. I was lying on my back with my hands under my head and my eyes half open. I knew it was time to get up, but I wanted to just doze for a minute before having to get out of bed. Suddenly there was a face dangling in front of me. It was like a mask on a string, hanging and bouncing over my bed. Only it was alive. The face was horrible looking, and it was laughing at me. I knew it was a demon, but I was so scared I didn't know what to

131

do. I tried to say the name of Jesus, but nothing came out. My lips were sealed. I tried to open my eyes, but they were glued shut. The face got closer and closer, laughing and laughing.

"I turned over on the bed and buried my head in the pillow, but the face was still in front of me. Dancing back and forth with a hollow, demonic laugh. Then I heard you and Mom moving around in the other room and the face gradually disappeared, laughing all the way."

"Why didn't you tell us?" I asked.

"I was too scared," Bruce confessed. "And then that night the earaches started and I forgot about the face until just a few minutes ago."

"Had you ever seen this face before?" I asked.

There was a long pause and then Bruce said softly, "Yes, sir. It is the same face on the back of that stereo album I bought last week."

I knew the album. I've always detested acid rock music, believing it was straight from the pit. But Bruce insisted on buying this album, saying that even though it was hard rock music, the words were religious.

"Where's the album?" I asked.

"In the closet," he said. "But Dad, you don't think it could be that, do you? I've only played it a couple of times and I really dig the music."

I got up and went to the closet. Finding the album I took it back to the bed. The jacket was covered with symbols, leering faces and twisting bodies. Every figure had a demonic connotation. It was as though the designer had taken a walk through hell and come back to paint what he saw.

"Get rid of it, Dad," Bruce said. "I never should have bought it."

Unlike idols which have been used in demon worship, I did not feel the album, or its horrible cover, were inherently demonic. By that, I mean I did not feel it was infested with

132

demons, or that by handling it one of them would "leap on me." However, I did see the album—and the jacket—as a tool through which Satan had pried open the door of the soul of a Spirit-baptized young man. Therefore I destroyed the record and the next morning the garbage men hauled it off to the dump—where it belonged.

But even this was not enough to set Bruce free from the splitting earaches. One of our church elders, Lew Draper, a former Southern Baptist pastor, was visiting at the house when Bruce came in from school the next afternoon. After a few moments conversation Bruce excused himself to go up to his room and study. After he left I told Lew of the strange events which had taken place.

Lew listened seriously and then said, "Where did Bruce listen to the music?"

"Up in his room," I said. "He knew we didn't approve of having that stuff played on our big stereo, so he used his small phonograph."

"Then we should exorcise the room," Lew said, rising to his feet. "It's not enough for Bruce to confess and repent. I believe the demons may still be present in the room and will probably attack him every time he lies down."

That sounded a bit strange to me, yet there had to be some reason Bruce was only bothered by the earaches at night, when he was alone in his room.

Lew and I went upstairs to Bruce's room, intent on cleansing it in the name of the Lord. When we got to the door I saw Bruce lying on his bed, his books spread open on the floor beside him. He was holding his head with his hands and twisting back and forth on the bed. The earaches had returned.

Lew didn't hesitate. He stepped into the room like David marching to meet Goliath. "In the name of the Son of God, the Lord Jesus Christ, I command you evil spirits to leave this room!" he roared.

Bruce came up off the bed like a spring had been released. Startled, he looked around and saw us standing there, hands in the air, vocally worshipping the Lord. Then we prayed for Bruce, asking God to bring inner healing to the wounds which had been caused by the presence of the demon, asking God to heal the memories and thereby close the door on fear. Finally, we bound the spirits so they could not return bringing guilt and doubt.

We sat and talked for a long time, but by the time Lew left, the earaches were gone. And they never returned.

By this deception of music young people are drawn under Satanic influence, without being aware of it. In Bruce's case, since he was a child of God, the attack was frontal. Satan actually tried to destroy him. In most cases the demons will not manifest themselves so vividly, preferring to work through the subtle attitudes of rebellion.

When I was working with Nicky Cruz on *Run Baby Run* he often spoke of the wild parties or ''jigs'' held by the gangs in Brooklyn. These were always accompanied by hard rock music. While the kids listened, they would be worked into a frenzy. Finally, driven by the demons into the streets, the boys would wildly strip parked cars, slash at their enemies with knives or tear up the shops along the sidewalk. Or, they would withdraw to the shadows of a basement to spend the afternoon in fornication. One member of Nicky's gang, the Mau Maus, told me, ''After listening to rock music there wasn't anything I wouldn't do.''

In his book, *What's Wrong with Rock and Roll,* Bob Larson says:

''The electronic insistence of guitars accompanied by the neurotic throbbing of drums compels the shedding of inhibitions . . . worst of all this music has become a religion. The message of rock and roll songs and performers is basically anti-Christian and opposed to Biblical standards of behavior.''

The noted district attorney, Vincent Bugliosi, who successfully tried and convicted Charles Manson and his ''family'' in the much publicized Sharon Tate murder trials in Los Angeles in the late 1960's, testified that Manson himself said he received his ideas by listening to music produced by the Beatles. In his book, *Helter Skelter,* Bugliosi quotes one of the family who said:

> ''Manson would quote, verbatim, whole lyrics from the Beatles' songs, finding in them a multitude of hidden meanings.''

Especially was Manson influenced by a Beatles' record on which the singers quoted frequently from passages in Revelation 9, accompanied by a weird drumbeat, throbbing electric guitar, and that musical mantra—the synthesizer. The fact that these tunes and records were composed and produced by men under the influence of drugs and transcendental meditation, was obviously the key to the Satanic power contained in the music.

While I was in the Philippines completing my research on *Into The Glory,* several missionaries told me I should interview Nard Pugyao. Nard was a young Isneg tribesman from the rugged mountains of northern Luzon. After his conversion to Christianity, members of the Wycliffe team had helped him get his education and then financed his trip to the United States where he received training as an aircraft mechanic at LeTourneau College in Longview, Texas. He then went on to the JAARS Center at Waxhaw, North Carolina, where he learned to fly. From there he planned to go to Moody Bible Institute in Chicago and finally, hopefully, to return to the Philippines as a JAARS pilot.

When I returned from the South Pacific, I looked up Nard in the hangar at Waxhaw Center. I had a new Hitachi tape recorder, one of the best machines on the market, and I wanted to ask Nard a few questions. He had been working on the engine of a small airplane, but put down his tools to chat for a few moments. During this time I discovered he had been raised in the tribal village by an aunt who was a *shaman,* a witch doctor. Intrigued, I flipped on my tape recorder and began to ask him questions about demon activity in the Philippines. He was reluctant to talk about it. When he became a Christian, he said, he had publicly renounced his heathen gods and been delivered from all demon influence. However, when I asked if he ever sensed any of the same demonic activity in the United States that he saw in the Philippine jungles, he said something of extreme interest.

"Demons never die, you know," he said matter-of-factly. "They just flit about from one place to another looking for someone who will invite them in. There are two places in America where I sense strong demon activity. One is around the pornography shops and theatres. My aunt, the *shaman,* used to take off her clothes to attract the demons. There is something in the American concept of nudity that invites demon spirits.

"The other is in rock music. In the tribe the witch doctor always used the heavy beat of drums to summon the demons. Today, here in America, when I hear rock music, I am aware it is a summons, an invitation, to the demons. It is the same beat we used in the Philippines."

We chatted awhile longer and then I returned to the administration building to meet with Bernie May, the executive director for JAARS. When I told him of my conversation with Nard he wrinkled his brow and said, "Well, I hope you got it on tape. No one else has been able to so far."

"What do you mean?"

"Nard has given that same testimony on three occasions in area churches, usually talking to young people," Bernie said. "Each time someone has tried to tape him, but something always goes wrong with the machine."

I grinned. "Well, I got it this time. I was watching the meter and it picked up everything."

Bernie looked at me seriously. "Did you pray, specifically, before you started the interview?"

"Well, no," I hesitated. "What difference should that make?"

"I don't think you're dealing with a normal force," Bernie said deliberately. "I think you'd better check, just to make sure."

I set my tape recorder on the table and pushed the rewind button. I ran the tape back to the middle of the interview, then clicked it into "play." The sound was perfect. Not only could I hear my questions and Nard's answers, but I could hear the sound of an airplane taking off on the nearby runway and the clink of tools as the mechanics worked in the hangar. I ran the tape forward to the place where we began talking about Nard's aunt, the *shaman*. Again the reception was perfect. I started to shut off the machine, but something happened. Suddenly, just as Nard began talking about the demons in the United States, the tape recorder went haywire. There were a series of "burping" sounds on the tape and suddenly it went into "Donald Duck talk"—wild gibberish. After that it faded out completely. Everything he had said about demons in America was gone.

I stood looking at Bernie. Neither of us said a word. He handed me his own tape recorder and we transferred the tape. Once again I ran it back to the beginning of this particular segment of the conversation and switched it into "play." The sounds were identical. It was as though some outside, magnetic force had deliberately interfered with the recording.

I put the tape back in my machine and switched it to "record." "Testing, one, two, three, four."

I flipped it to "rewind," then back to "play." The sound was perfect. Only that portion about demons was unintelligible.

137

My conclusion: the demons simply did not want that conversation recorded.

To this day most of those who are converted to Christ in heathen cultures know they must burn their fetishes and household gods, turn their back on all demon attractions and submit themselves to deliverance from all demonic possession. This entails severing all connections with the occult and music of their former religions, and avoiding all demonic cult festivals and sites. Christ will not associate with that which is inspired by the enemy.

> *Don't be teamed with those who do not love the Lord, for what do the people of God have in common with the people of sin? How can light live with darkness? And what harmony can there be between Christ and the devil? How can a Christian be a partner with one who doesn't believe? And what union can there be between God's temple and idols? For you are God's temple, the home of the living God, and God has said of you, "I will live in them and walk among them, and I will be their God and they shall be my people. That is why the Lord has said, "Leave them, separate yourselves from them; don't touch their filthy things, and I will welcome you, and be a Father to you, and you will be my sons and daughters (II Corinthians 6:14-18 LB).*

The methods of deliverance are as many and as varied as the methods of possession and oppression. I personally believe that a dynamic conversion experience should include total deliverance from the powers of darkness. In my own case, though, my conversion was not dynamic or total. Thus my experience of the baptism in the Holy Spirit also brought about deliverance. Likewise, when I was baptized in water there was additional deliverance. Some need to go through deliverance sessions which will certainly contain confession, repentance and perhaps even rebuking certain demons. Occasionally in our Sunday morning worship services, as we move into high praise, a demon will manifest himself and we will have to take immediate authority over it to keep it from disrupting the service or tearing some poor person's body. There is no set pattern, but the authority always rests in the name of Jesus Christ.

One evening, after Corrie ten Boom had spoken at our church, she was approached by a young lady who had been involved in witchcraft. Corrie took immediate authority over the demons and commanded them to leave in the name of Jesus. The girl was instantly set free. Afterwards Jackie asked Tante Corrie what method she used in deliverance. Corrie looked at her sternly and said, ''I do it however the Lord tells me to do it.''

And that settled the matter.

It must be remembered that Satan is a defeated foe. He has no authority, no right, to possess the soul of a Christian—or to leave his demons behind to do his dirty work. The only authority he has is that which we give him. Once he is ordered from the premises in the name of the Lord Jesus Christ, he is compelled to leave—and take his vexing spirits with him. Healing of the inner man may be necessary to patch up the wounds he caused, but in all areas, Jesus is victor.

8

GETTING YOUR MOTIVES STRAIGHT

The Lamplighter Cafeteria in Ft. Myers, Florida, was humming with activity when I arrived to go through the evening serving line. I was to speak at the monthly meeting of the Full Gospel Business Men's Fellowship and had been instructed that after I ate, I was to meet with the believers in a side room.

It was the heart of the winter tourist season and most of the people in the cafeteria were of retirement age. The same proved true when I joined the group in the side room for the time of fellowship. In fact, looking around, it seemed I was the youngest person in the meeting.

We sang a few songs, there were some testimonies, and then, just before I spoke, the president announced a special musical number by the chapter's "senior duet." Everybody present seemed to know the two old men who stood to sing, so I sat back and relaxed, trying to collect my thoughts before I stood to speak.

But it was impossible to collect my thoughts. The two men, both of them well into their retirement years, were accompanying themselves musically. One was playing a guitar, the other a banjo with only three strings. One string had been missing for a year, he apologized, and the other had broken while he was trying to tune the instrument just before the meeting. To make matters worse, the three remaining strings were out of tune. But so was the guitar, so it didn't make much difference.

After some preliminary plunking and strumming, trying to get the instruments in tune, the men gave up and began to sing. "When They Ring Those Golden Bells for You and Me."

It was bad. They started, one of them singing lead and the other tenor, and then stopped. They decided to change parts and started again, this time with both of them singing lead. Finally, after an embarrassing exchange of comments over who was to sing which part, they began a third time—both of them singing tenor. Undaunted, they painfully strummed and plucked their way through the first verse,

There's a land beyond the river,

That we call the sweet forever . . .

Half way through the chorus another string on the banjo popped with a loud twang. This disconcerted the old man who was plucking. He forgot the words and started singing something else.

I could hardly believe what I was hearing. I shuddered, embarrassed for them, embarrassed for the visitors present, and mortified that I was being identified with it all.

I tried to close my ears. I tried to think how I could overcome this horrible presentation when I stood to speak. It was, without doubt, the worst musical presentation I had ever heard. Yet the old men went on and on, oblivious of my red face and twitching hands.

"God help us," I moaned inwardly.

Then, just as clear as the sound of those golden bells the old men were singing about, He answered me in the deep place of my heart.

"You think that sounds pretty awful, don't you?"

"Oh, God, you know," I groaned.

"Would you like to know what I think about it?" He said gently.

I felt the hair begin to rise on the back of my neck. I had the feeling I had ventured out into an area where I had absolutely no business being. I was afraid to answer, afraid He would tell me what He thought.

It didn't make any difference. He told me anyway. "Those are two of my choicest saints. They stand and sing, knowing their voices are cracked and their instruments out of tune, because they love Me. They are singing to My glory, and I have commanded all the angels in Heaven to be quiet so I can hear them."

I could hardly breathe. "Oh, God, what a fool I am. I was listening with *my* ears, rather than Yours."

"That's right," He chided me gently. "Not only that, but you were judging them by worldly standards, while I was judging them by kingdom standards. You were listening to *how* they sang. I was listening to *why* they sang."

One of the primary reasons we are unable to enter into inner healing is we have never learned the importance of getting our motives straight. As a result we develop ulcers, bad attitudes, and grouchy dispositions as we strive to complete a task which we outwardly proclaim is for God's glory, but for which, inwardly, we plan to take the credit.

God, I have discovered, is far more concerned over *why* we do a thing than *how* we do it. The person who demands perfection at any cost has paid too high a price. If two old men with cracked voices and out-of-tune instruments can cause God to hush the angels so He can listen, it seems the rest of us better do some deep checking of our own reasons for singing, preaching, writing, publishing, raising children, earning money, or anything else we glibly proclaim we are doing for the glory of God.

My first introduction to the importance of motives came on the publication of my first book, *Run Baby Run*. I really thought my motives were pure when I signed my contract with Logos International. Oh, sure, I enjoyed being introduced as a "professional writer." But at least I wasn't in it for the money. In fact, it never occurred to me until much, much later that there might be some financial rewards connected to writing. I was satisfied just to "get the word out"—and to be known all over the world as the man who wrote the book.

Having already determined that He was going to bring me into the image of His Son, God decided to go to work with His sandpaper on that particular motive. When the book was finally published, Logos sent me the first copy via air mail, special delivery. It arrived on a Saturday morning when the entire family was at home. Jackie and the children eagerly crowded around as I ripped off the wrapping paper and exposed that brilliant red dust jacket with the name across the middle: *Run Baby Run*.

We passed the book around. Everyone handled it—or perhaps "fondled" is a better word—looking at the type, the art work on the cover, the thickness of the pages, and the personal inscription written in longhand and signed by the publisher, thanking me for my part in the book.

But I was disappointed. Nicky Cruz's name was emblazoned in big letters across the top of the book. At the bottom of the front cover was Billy Graham's name, also in big letters, since he had written the Foreword. And in the middle, in very small type, it said, "As told to Jamie Buckingham."

Our number two girl, Bonnie, looked at the book and said, "Daddy, your name isn't very big, is it?"

I blushed and tried to explain that I was an unknown writer, that the book was actually about Nicky's life, that they needed Billy's endorsement to catch the eye of the bookstore owners, and besides, I had written the book to the glory of God. In fact, it really didn't make any difference whether my name appeared at all—as long as God knew about it.

But it did make a difference. It made a whopping difference. That afternoon I took the book into my studio, closed the door, and sat for a long time—looking at the cover. It didn't seem right. After all, I was the fellow who had done all the work. I was the one who had taken time away from my family, my ministry, and a lot of other things to struggle to get the words on paper. I was even the one who had convinced Billy Graham to write the Foreword. Why then was my name so small and everyone else's so large?

It's the same syndrome that affects a lot of executives in business when they *demand* their own parking stall—with their name on the curb—or their own coat closet. It's the thing that causes ministers to *demand* their name on the sign in front of the church, painted on the side of the church bus, or their picture on their stationery with a list of their various degrees. It's that thing in us that demands recognition, even when we say we're giving God the glory. It's called a sick inner nature and is caused by emptiness. Only the inner security brought about by the filling of the Holy Spirit will bring healing.

How well I remembered a former church I had pastored which went through a building program to renovate the auditorium. The money ran out just before they got the new pews paid for. The finance committee, playing on this sick area of man's inner nature, raised the money for the new pews by promising the people that anyone who contributed $350 would get their name on one of the long pews (on a little bronze plaque) while $250 would purchase a plaque on a short pew. They raised the money for all sixty-six pews in less than a month.

I had highly criticized that syndrome back then—feeling

the action of the committee, while it proved successful, was really feeding a sickness rather than helping to bring people into spiritual maturity. Now I was caught in the same web, only this time it wasn't my name on a church pew, but on the cover of a book.

It took me almost a month to get over the hurt and disappointment sufficiently to hear God again. But as the wound began to heal, I realized God had allowed it to happen to teach me about the inner nature of man. Success corrupts. Proclaim a man famous, and apart from the grace of God, it will destroy him. Give a man a title, and suddenly his personality begins to change.

We discovered this much later in our church when we decided it was time to establish elders and deacons. As long as we didn't have any titled leaders, the people in the body were flowing with the Spirit, ministering to each other and generally enjoying their fellowship with God and one another. Then we decided to formally recognize our leaders and vest them with titles. There was nothing wrong with that, we just moved too soon, before the men were healed enough so they wouldn't revert to their former traditions, or start acting on the basis of reaction rather than responding to the Holy Spirit. Soon our new deacons were acting like old deacons, and our elders began to act like they thought elders should act. Before long we had not only a "clergy" but a "hierarchy." It was the old problem of being placed in a position without first holding authority. It took us almost two years to undo that mistake, drop all the titles, and start over again (with some of the same men, incidentally), placing the emphasis on leaders being servants rather than dictators.

I could have my name in big letters on my books if I wanted. All I had to do was storm the publisher's office, make a nuisance of myself, demand my rights, and I'd get them.

I was chagrined over my attitude and found myself praying

what I now realize is one of the most dangerous prayers in the kingdom. I prayed, "Lord, I want to be a seed that falls into the ground and dies."

Seeds, of course, can never reproduce unless they die. The only way they die is to be buried in the ground, covered with dirt, and then sprinkled with manure. Had I known all that, I might not have prayed that prayer, but I was determined to get my motives straight. I was sick of being motivated by selfish, sick things that belched out of my subconscious like brimstone out of a volcano. I wanted to be pure, and the only way I knew how was to die to self.

As usual, God immediately put me to the test. My second book was written for Kathryn Kuhlman—and my name didn't even appear on the dust jacket.

There is another story that surrounded the writing of that book, by the way. Dan Malachuk introduced me to Miss Kuhlman in her offices of the Carlton House in Pittsburgh, Pennsylvania. I knew almost nothing about her except that she had one book published called *I Believe in Miracles,* that she was involved in a healing and miracle ministry. She turned out to be one of the most gracious, charming, and genuine women I had ever met.

We went out to eat that night in a quaint little steak house overlooking the Ohio River. After dinner, Miss Kuhlman, whom I soon discovered was an astute businesswoman as well as a person of great spiritual power, got right to the point. Was I willing to write her next book? Yes. How long did I think it would take? I estimated two months if I worked full time. (I sadly underestimated—it took six months.) How would I like to get paid?

I paused here for I knew almost nothing about the financial arrangements in book publishing. Miss Kuhlman was patient and explained that I had a choice. I could either draw a royalty on each book as it was sold or she would be willing to pay me a flat fee—whatever I thought was fair.

As usual we were in a tight financial situation. The little church in Florida was still struggling and I saw this as an opportunity to go off salary for a couple of months, give the church a chance to catch up financially, and at the same time get paid for writing. I did some quick mental arithmetic and determined I would need $1,000 a month to support my family for the two-month period it should take me to write the book. This was $200 a month more than the church was able to pay me, but I thought it seemed fair to draw a little extra since this was a special project.

I took a deep breath and told Miss Kuhlman I would write the book for $2,000. It was more money than I had ever asked anyone for in a lump sum.

She gave me a funny look and said, "Is that enough?"

"Yes, ma'am," I said, sensing that she was willing to go along with my offer.

"You feel you would be more comfortable with the flat fee rather than a royalty?" she asked.

I nodded. I was determined to write that book for the glory of God and was satisfied to get paid just enough to support my family and buy typing paper.

Miss Kuhlman smiled and patted my arm. "I'll have my secretary write you a check next week." I left, feeling like I was the richest man in the world.

Funny thing about the book. It sold almost 400,000 copies the first year in the hardback edition. At $5 a copy, that added up to a gross sales of $2 million. A co-author's royalties on such sales would have amounted to many times more than the $2,000 I asked for.

For those living in the kingdom of God and who desire inner healing, there are some mysterious economic absurdities which open the doors to vast intangible riches and a deep inner satisfaction.

They are:

> *The first shall be last and the last shall be first.*
> *You are allowed to keep only that which you give away.*
> *In order to live, you have to die. To get high, stay low.*

The blessing of that single experience with *God Can Do It Again* has extended far beyond me to my family and church. It was unexpected and unasked for. In fact, had I entered into the project for that purpose, I would have been automatically disqualified. We are not to ever undertake a project for the purpose of receiving God's blessing—whether it is tithing our income, teaching a class, or giving our lives to go to the mission field. The only adequate motive for any project is "for the glory of God." Choose any other motive and you run the risk of receiving your reward here.

9

RELEASE FROM TYRANNY

One of the most critical of all relationships is the one we have with our parents. As strange as it may seem, for many of us this relationship does not need strengthening; rather it needs loosing. Too often our ties to father and mother actually form a bondage which enslaves us to the tyranny of ancestry and prevents us from entering into the single relationship with our Heavenly Father which brings inner healing.

This principle is vividly illustrated in a story from the Old Testament. Following the death of King Solomon, the kingdom of Israel was divided into two sections: Judah in the south and Israel in the north. There followed a line of kings, most of them so wicked they actually forbade the people to worship God. One of these was Ahaz.

Ahaz inherited the throne at the age of twenty and immediately came under the influence of men from Assyria who offered to help him fight the Philistines. Soon he was worshiping the idols the Assyrians brought from Damascus. Not only did he sacrifice to them, but he set up altars under every tree in Israel, and required the people to worship the "devas," the evil spirits. He also set up stone altars and sacrificed children to the evil spirits, some of his own children included. In the final years of his life he was so obsessed with evil that he even took the sacred vessels from the house of the Lord and gave them to the Assyrians. He nailed shut the doors of the Temple and proclaimed it an offense, punishable by death, for anyone to worship Jehovah.

It takes a great deal to make the Lord—the God of lovingkindness and mercy—angry. But the Bible says Ahaz was so wicked he "provoked to anger the Lord God of his fathers." He died, at the age of thirty-six, in a mad rage against God. The priests would not allow him to be buried in the royal tombs.

Ahaz had a son, a young teenager, who was destined to succeed him as king of Israel. There is no record of who raised young Hezekiah from the time his wicked father died until he inherited the crown. Perhaps it was the same people who denied his father burial in the royal tombs. We don't know. But when he was twenty-five, Hezekiah was crowned king of Israel.

Something had happened, though, between the time his father died and the time he became king. Hezekiah had turned from the ways of his father and developed a deep love for God. In fact, when he was crowned, his first official act was to open the doors of the House of the Lord and to repair the Temple which his father had tried to destroy. Aside from Josiah, his great-grandson, and King David, the Bible records no more godly king in the history of Israel than Hezekiah.

The Hebrews placed a strong emphasis on family ties. Jews did not even have a last name, but were simply known as "the son of." Peter, that great disciple of Jesus, was first known

as Simon bar Jonah, the Aramaic word *bar* meaning "son of."
The fifth of the ten commandments is the only commandment
that contains a promise:

> *Honour thy father and thy mother: that thy days may
> be long upon the land which the Lord thy God giveth thee
> (Exodus 21:12).*

From the very beginning of Hebrew history the people put
great stock in their ancestral lineage, their heritage—especially
as it related to their father. Yet something had happened to
Hezekiah which gave him the courage and the wisdom to break
loose from this tyranny and hear the voice of God. In his
opening speech to the priests and Levites, he called them into
the open space east of the Temple and addressed them, saying,

> *Sanctify yourselves, and sanctify the house of the
> Lord God of your fathers, and carry forth the filthiness out
> of the holy place. For our fathers have trespassed, and
> done that which was evil in the eyes of the Lord our God
> and have forsaken him, and have turned away their faces
> from the habitation of the Lord, and turned their backs.
> . . . Now it is in mine heart to make a covenant with the
> Lord God of Israel, that his fierce wrath may turn away
> from us (2 Chronicles 29:5, 6, 10).*

In the ears of many of the people this must have sounded as
blasphemous as the words of his father when he commanded
them to close the Temple and worship idols. For any man, even
the king, to stand and confess that his father had sinned and led
them into a place of destruction and shame was tantamount to
denying God Himself. Yet not only did Hezekiah proclaim his
own father had sinned, but he said the fathers of the others had

sinned also, and it was time to make a break and start afresh with God. He was, literally, renouncing an entire generation of fathers. What an amazing and bold statement for a young man to make as he begins his political career.

However, once the spiritual bondage of his father was broken, Hezekiah was free to hear from God in a way that no king had heard since David. He instituted many new reforms. When the Levites could not get the Temple purified in time for the April Passover, Hezekiah changed the date of the Passover to May—something that no king, or priest, had ever dared do before. Not only that, but when it became obvious the people could not go through the lengthy but necessary purification rites in time to meet the Passover deadline, Hezekiah lined them up and said, "May the good Lord pardon everyone who determines to follow the Lord God of his fathers, even though he is not properly sanctified for the ceremony." The priests were horrified, and fully expected the young king to be struck dead. But to their amazement, the Lord listened to Hezekiah's prayer and honored his enthusiasm.

Having broken the tyranny of his father, he was also able to break senseless traditions. He was able to hear from God in a new way and for a number of years led the people to fresh commitments to the living Lord. In the end, after a long and noble reign, he died and was buried with great honors in the royal tombs in Jerusalem.

The story of Hezekiah is one of the most fascinating in the Bible—not only because of the conflict and change in his life, but because it contains some of the vital principles of inner healing. In particular, Hezekiah shows us that honoring our parents should not put us in bondage.

For years I was disturbed by Jesus' reaction to the men who approached him while he was teaching in the synagogue and said his mother and his brothers were waiting for him outside.

Jesus' answer seemed so blunt:

> *My mother and my brethren are these which hear the word of God and do it (Luke 8:21).*

In another place He said:

> *If any man come to me, and hate not his father, and mother, and wife, and children, and brethren, and sisters, yea, and his own life also, he cannot be my disciple (Luke 14:26).*

How can we honor our father and mother and hate them at the same time? Could it be that Jesus was drawing a comparison and saying that the highest honor we can pay father and mother is to give our first allegiance to the Lord? In fact, that allegiance should be so strong that in comparison, our love for our parents would seem like hate.

Many of us are under bondage to our ancestors: father and mother, grandparents, uncles, aunts, or even older brothers and sisters. We may call the relationship love, but, if it keeps us from inner healing, it is really sentimentalism—a tyranny which exerts a far greater bondage upon our minds than the chains of a prison.

In 1800, Thomas Jefferson wrote to Dr. Benjamin Rush and set forth his political concepts for the Republic. He said:

> I have sworn upon the altar of God, eternal hostility against every form of tyranny over the mind of man.

Jefferson's hatred of this kind of bondage was repeated in another letter, written sixteen years later to his friend Dupont de Nemours, where he stated:

> Enlighten the people, generally, and tyranny and oppressions of body and mind will vanish like evil spirits at the dawn of day.

Jefferson's solution to political tyranny—enlightenment—has deep spiritual significance as well. The old saying that "love is blind" often means that love causes us to go blind, preventing us from seeing objectively. Of course such "love" is not really love at all, but sentimentality. But the blindness is just as real.

Many a father, even though he says he loves his children, has played the role of a tyrant by binding his children to him in an unnatural way.

A dear friend of ours, Thelma, recently went through a tragic divorce. Thelma was still a teenager when her mother died. Her father, who was then in his fifties, went into a period of mourning which lasted twenty years. As the only girl in the family (there were three sons, all married), Thelma felt obligated to stay home and take care of her father. Across the years she had brief flings at romance, but somehow her father always managed to break things up. He didn't do it by violence, but by playing on his daughter's sympathy. "I need you with me, Thelma. I don't think I can face life without you now that Mother is gone."

Then, when Thelma was thirty-four, she met a fine young man who seemed to understand her situation. A widower with four small children, he was patient as he courted her. When she called to say she had to break a date because her father was "sick," he understood. When she told him she could marry him only if he could provide for her father, he agreed. They were married in a small church wedding and Thelma and her father moved from the old home place to live with her husband in a nearby town.

The first year was happy. Thelma seemed to be making the

necessary adjustments and the children responded well to her natural love. But then Thelma's father began to miss the old house. He begged Thelma to let him return home, where he could "die in peace." It broke her heart, but she finally agreed, believing her place was with her husband, but her father could not turn loose. Once home, he began to call. There was no one there to take care of him, he complained. He was afraid he would have a stroke and be alone in the house, helpless, for days before anyone found him. He never asked her to come home, his tyranny was far more subtle. He just played on her heartstrings until she finally returned to take care of him. "It will be for just a short while," she told her husband.

But once home she fell into the old routine and, unable to escape the bondage, finally wrote her husband and told him she could not leave her father to die alone. Brokenhearted, she asked him to get a divorce. She was not coming back. "I'm too bound to the past to change," she said.

How does one break the bondage of ancestral ties and find release from tyranny? The answer to this, as to all questions concerning inner healing, is found in the Bible. In this case we need look no farther than the life of Hezekiah.

The tragedy of sentimental love is that it blinds us from reality, preventing us from seeing the truth about our family relationships. Thus the first principle of release is to look at our situation objectively.

After the death of Ahaz, Hezekiah was able to step back and look at the situation from a distance He was able to see that even though he had been taught to honor his father, nevertheless his father was a godless man.

True love does not hide its head in the sand, it enables us to look facts square in the face. Confessing that his father was godless did not cause Hezekiah to love him any less. In fact, it should have caused him to love him more. It is sentimentality which binds us to the facts and prevents us from acting objectively. True love will bring enlightenment which will, as Jefferson rightly ascertained, cause "tyranny and oppressions of the body and mind" to "vanish like evil spirits at the dawn of day."

The call of Christ is for the people of God to take authority over the bondage of ancestry—of those both living and dead—and "quit ye like men, be strong." We should rebuke any spirit that tells us we should not look honestly at all our family relationships. We need to see the weaknesses of our parents, as well as their strengths. Much of our godlessness is inherited, either consciously or unconsciously, from our ancestors. In fact, there is a type of generic bondage which extends all the way back to Adam—a bondage which is inherited from those long dead yet is a strong reality in our lives. It is such a generic relationship which not only causes us, occasionally, to look like a great, great grandparent—but even to act like him.

Release from such tyranny is found by following Hezekiah's example—making a personal covenant with God and renouncing the false idols of our fathers.

Hezekiah said:

> *I have made a covenant with the Lord God of Israel . . . to stand before him, to serve him, and that ye should minister unto him, and burn incense (2 Chronicles 29:10,11).*

This was an open declaration that he would not serve the god of his father, whoever that god might be, but would only serve the true and living God.

In all probability, your parents never built an altar under a tree, sacrificed children, or bowed down before stone idols. But every one of us is guilty of having built altars which were not of God. A young man in our church stood one night and confessed the bondage he had to his father. His father had never been able to pay his bills. An itinerant construction worker, he had moved from one community to another amassing huge debts. When his creditors came to repossess what he had bought, he would move on. As a result, this young fellow grew up watching his father pay homage to the god of money. Every decision was based on finances. If the family moved, it was because the father could get a better job somewhere else with more money, or because his creditors were forcing him to leave. The idea of hearing from God and following His direction was as foreign as flying to the moon.

The young man finally left home and joined a motorcycle gang. Eventually he wound up in our town and, somehow, came in contact with several young Christians. Through their influence he, too, became a Christian. When he did, his violent ways changed and he became a gentle, affectionate young man who soon found a sweet young lady and married her.

However, despite the tremendous change in his personality, the bondage of the past was still with him. Some of the elders in the church began receiving complaints from the local merchants. The merchants knew he was a member of the church because he openly testified of his faith in Christ. But he could not handle his money. He was deeply in debt, following the same path his father had taken. He had run up huge accounts with his credit cards, had purchased luxuries (such as a color TV) which he could not afford, and had finally gone to a loan shark who was now threatening to take him to court.

Some of the more mature men in church perceived that his problem stemmed from a bondage to his father. They counseled him and it wasn't long before he stood on a Sunday night and renounced the tyranny that carried over from his childhood. He made a public covenant with God that he would no longer serve the gods of his father. Following the advice of his spiritual counselors, he tore up all his credit cards, sold or sent back everything he didn't need, and entered a program of disciplined spending. It took more than a year for him to get out of the hole, but now he is operating in the black, saving money in order to pay cash for furniture and the like.

Only God knows the bondage we put on our children. An old friend of mine tells of the first forty years of her life and says it was like living in hell—even though her entire life was spent in church and the last fifteen years of it as a foreign missionary nurse in Africa.

As far back as she could remember, her mother had told her she was to be a foreign missionary. The mother even went so far as to say God had told her she would serve in Africa. Ignorant of spiritual matters, she didn't know such a call should come only from God, directly.

The young lady dutifully went to college, nursing school, and seminary—preparing for her career as a missionary. Yet deep inside she knew it was not God, but mother, who was directing her life. It took fifteen years in Nigeria before she finally came to herself and realized she was out of God's will. She resigned from the foreign mission board of her denomination and returned home.

Her action broke her mother's heart. As long as her daughter was a missionary in Africa, the mother had enjoyed a special type of respect in her local church. Others knew her as the "missionary's mother." But now that her daughter had resigned as a missionary, "left the ministry" so to speak, the mother was crushed.

Eventually the mother confessed that when she, herself, was a young girl, God had spoken to her and nudged her toward the mission field. Instead, she had married early and followed her husband to the Midwest rather than Africa. When she discovered she was pregnant, she promised God if he would give her a daughter she would dedicate her to the task originally asked of the mother, that of being a foreign missionary. But in the "dedication" she had bound the child to a false call—and effectively blocked her from hearing God's voice in her own life.

However, after all those years, the daughter was finally free. She took a job at a hospital and is now the director of nurses' training. Ironically, some of the girls in her classes are preparing for the mission field and she is a great help to them. But she, herself, will never go back. That was her mother's call, not hers.

Bondage to parents and their ideals can come in many ways. Even our "confessions" bind a child. Countless numbers of children have been established in life patterns by parents who called them "dumbbells." One man says he grew up with a worthless concept of himself because his father, time and time again, said, "You'll never amount to anything. You'll always be a troublemaker."

Actually that confession was a curse which followed him throughout all the years of his life. The boy eventually wound up in prison remembering—and hating—the curse put on him by his father.

Such curses are not easily broken. As in the case of Hezekiah, it often takes a public declaration that you will no longer recognize the godless ways of a parent, but will submit only to the direction of the heavenly Father. Since this crosses the grain of all that we esteem honorable and noble, since it breaks the chains of sentimentality, it is extremely difficult. But often it is the only way we can gain release from tyranny and move into inner healing.

There are other altars at which our parents have worshiped which need to be renounced. Altars of expediency, self, and pride. Or perhaps it was an altar to some kind of family heritage. As a boy I can remember my father grilling me, saying, "Remember, you are a Buckingham. Never do anything which will bring disgrace to the family name."

After my father became a Christian I never heard him talk about the "family name." However, I often heard him refer to the fact that I was a child of the King and an ambassador of Jesus Christ. "Remember," he said, "you carry the banner of the Lord wherever you go. You are the only Bible some people will read. Represent your Lord well."

All sons are not as fortunate as I, however. Many boys and girls grow up having been taught to worship at the altar under the family tree. In animal husbandry a pure blood line is referred to as a "thoroughbred." Tragically, that concept often extends from dogs and horses to the human race, until people take great pride in who their ancestors are, claiming some kind of present position based on the fact that their uncle was a bishop or their grandfather a governor. We use the term "blue blood" to give us status which is supposedly inherited through the lineage.

There are, in America and the United Kingdom, investigative companies who do nothing but trace family trees, redesign coats of arms, or determine which totem or tartan represents our clan. The altars we build under these family trees are just as real as the altars Ahaz built under the trees in Israel. We dote on our heritage, and in many homes huge pictures of ancestors stare down at us as we eat, study, sleep, or procreate. It's no wonder that our offspring grow up in such bondage to the past. Organizations such as the Daughters of the American Revolution and Daughters of the Confederacy, as well as many fraternal organizations were formed to perpetuate the ancestral heritage or keep the race lines "pure." Such bondage is often a curse.

Others may not trace the family tree back to the Mayflower but take great pride in saying, "My granddaddy built this church," or "Our family have always been Catholics."

My first church after I left seminary was a large, old, downtown congregation in a textile community in South Carolina. Pride in tradition and family heritage ran deep. The church was ruled by a small handful of people who had inherited their power from their fathers. Men were elected to important positions in the church on the basis of their ancestral line rather than their relationship with the Father. Many of the families occupied the same pew on Sunday morning as their forefathers had occupied. To consider changing, or sharing, was as unthinkable as swapping wives.

One Sunday morning I took my usual place on the platform and looked over the congregation at a strange sight. The sanctuary was laid out with three sections of pews extending from front to back. The long pews in the middle row held twelve people each, while the short pews on both sides were five-seaters. A professor, his wife, and three old maid sisters who lived with them had occupied the same pew—one of the five-seaters—for many years. It was the same pew, or at least in the same vicinity (since we had recently renovated the sanctuary), that his father had occupied before him. In fact, there was a bronze plaque on the end of the pew that had his name, his wife's name, and the names of the three sisters, indicating he had "donated" $250 which went to purchase a pew in the newly renovated church—no doubt that very one.

No one ever sat in the professor's pew but the professor. If he or his family were sick, or for some reason—which was rare indeed—missed the church service, the pew always remained vacant in his honor.

But on that particular Sunday morning when I took my place on the platform, seven people were crowded into the professor's five-person pew. The professor, his wife, and the three sisters were there—along with a couple I had never seen before. They looked absolutely absurd, squeezed into that tiny bench in obvious discomfort, maybe even pain. It was even stranger since there were plenty of empty seats close by.

It wasn't until after the service that one of the ushers told me what had happened. The professor had been late arriving that morning and somehow a visiting couple had inadvertently slipped into "their" pew. When the professor arrived, rather than taking another seat or splitting up his clan so part of them could sit one place and the rest in their usual place, they all squeezed in on the visiting couple and remained there throughout the service.

The bondage of the past was too great to break. Tradition, established by the tyranny of ancestry, was more powerful than comfort or change.

Such ancestor worship is not only foolish, it is idolatrous. Paul says when a man becomes a new creature in Christ old things are passed away; behold all things are become new (2 Corinthians 5:17).

From that time on, family trees, national heritage, traditions, "blood lines," and titles should mean nothing. For centuries people have justified their immature behavior and volatile personalities by blaming it on their ancestral traditions.

"All us redheads blow our stacks sometimes."

"He's just like his father, always chasing after women."

"Every woman in that family has been lazy."

"I can't help it. My mother was the same way."

Such excuses are not only contrary to the theology of the Bible, but actually become curses we place on each other—and on ourselves.

Equally devastating is our determination to convince ourselves, and others, that we are locked into a personality pattern by our nationality—a trait that millions of people accept with great pride.

"I know I lose my temper, but I'm Irish."

"Sure I'm stubborn. So are all Dutchmen."

"Those Germans are always so precise."

"I can't help it if I'm emotional. I'm Italian."

"I sure wouldn't let my daughter go out with a Frenchman."

"Never trust an Arab."

"If you were a Jew, and your ancestors had been persecuted like mine, you'd be bitter also."

"All Scots are stingy."

But I'm not a Scotchman, even though my ancestors were born there. I am a child of God. What difference does it make whether one's ancestors were murdered by the Nazis, killed by the Japanese, raped by the Yankees or slaughtered by the Confederates. When a person becomes a new creature in Christ old things pass away. From that time on the only "blood line" we have bypasses the Mayflower, it even bypasses father Abraham, and flows directly from the Father through His Son. It does not extend back to Ireland, or Italy or Russia. We have literally inherited a new character—the character of our heavenly Father.

In early 1974 I sat in on a press conference in Jerusalem prior to the First World Conference on the Holy Spirit. During the conference it was apparent the Jewish reporters were far more interested in finding the political opinions of the speakers, than their spiritual concerns. When the answers were not forthcoming, a militant Jewish reporter turned to a Christian Arab pastor who was part of the local planning committee and asked, "Tell me, pastor, who do you think owns this land—the Jews or the Arabs?"

It was a baited question, the same kind thrown at Jesus 2,000 years before. Yet the same Holy Spirit who imparted supernatural wisdom to the Son of God, inspired this Arab believer.

"I was born to hate Jews," he said in halting English. "I was taught from birth this land was ours and we should take it at any cost. Then Jesus Christ, the Jewish Messiah and Savior of the world, entered my heart. Since that time I no longer quibble over the rocks and sand of this land. I am but a pilgrim passing through on my way to a new home prepared for me beyond Jordan. This is not my land—or yours—it is God's."

There was a long moment of silence. Then the Jewish reporter—with just a trace of moisture in his eyes—slowly rose to his feet and began to slowly clap his hands in applause. There were no more questions.

In Jesus Christ we literally inherit a new ancestry. The old root which formerly extended deep into our traditions, our heritage, our family tree, is hacked off, and the indwelling Holy Spirit now sends our roots deep into the rich soil on the banks of the River of Life.

Sidney Lanier caught that spirit as he wandered through the Marshes of Glynn near Brunswick, Georgia. He wrote:

As the marsh-hen secretly builds on the watery sod,
Behold I will build me a nest on the greatness of God;
I will fly in the greatness of God as the marsh-hen flies
In the freedom that fills all the space 'twixt the marsh and
the skies:
By so many roots as the marsh-grass sends in the sod
I will heartily lay me a-hold on the greatness of God.

It should make no more difference whether we had oriental parents, if our great-uncle was a Prussian baron, or if we come from a long line of Ku Klux Klanners. Once we are reborn into Christ, our ancestry is traced to the cross; our traditions are no longer bound in the old wineskins of the church, culture, or community, but take on the change of new wine; and it makes no difference, even if our ancestors were lords, earls, dukes, or kings, for now we are heirs to a far greater throne, joint heirs with the Son of God Himself.

In the Bible the change was so often so dramatic, so literal, that the people underwent an actual change of name. In the case of Simon bar Jonah (Simon, son of Jonah), for instance, Jesus said that from that time on his name would be Simon Peter. No longer was ancestry linked to the sandy soil of an earthly heritage, but built upon the solid rock of the eternal Father in heaven.

Abram (exalted father) became who he actually was, *Abraham* (father of multitudes). The covenant relationship with God was literally built into his new name. *Jacob,* the trickster, became *Israel,* the soldier of God. And *Saul,* who longed to be great in the eyes of the world, became *Paul,* a name which means little and humble.

My own name is James William Buckingham II, indicating that I was named after my grandfather on my father's side, who was also James William Buckingham. However, my mother, whose Thompson family hailed from Wales and Scotland, had a penchant for Scottish names. Therefore, from the very beginning I was both James William and "Jamie." I grew up disliking both names. James William reminded me of my grandfather who died before I was born. I can remember standing for long moments staring up at his musty picture in that great oval frame which hung in the attic, wondering if I would grow up to look like him—string tie, black bowler derby, and all.

On the other hand, I winced every time I heard the name Jamie. Maybe it was the sound of my mother's voice calling out the back door, "Jaa-mee!" Perhaps it was the fact that there were two girls in my second grade class named Jamie (some of my friends said Jamie was a feminine name). I've often wondered just how much this reaction affected my life and drove me on to ruinous efforts to try to prove my masculinity when it didn't need proving at all. When my high school girl friend bought me a silver ID bracelet for Christmas one year, I asked her to have the engraver use my initials, "J. W. Buckingham" rather than "Jamie Buckingham."

But even so, my motives were not pure. I was doing it to prove something to myself, and it wasn't until after I allowed

Jesus Christ to take the reins of my life that I was free to accept my name. I didn't have to prove whatever it was I thought I had to prove. I belonged to His family and just as He had redeemed my nature and my body, so He had redeemed my name. Since then there has been real peace in simply being "Jamie." And when the mail sometimes comes addressed to Miss Jamie Buckingham (just as my wife's mail sometimes comes addressed to Mr. Jackie Buckingham), I no longer feel resentment or even embarrassment. I'm free.

Last year I spent a few days in Japan with a small group of Christians from Kyoto. One of those in the group was the pastor of a Southern Baptist Church. He gave me some additional insight into the problem of ancestor worship, which of course is deeply ingrained in many orientals.

It is not uncommon, he said, for a Japanese to become a Christian, join the church, learn the hymns, read his Bible, bring his children to Sunday school, and even serve as an officer in the church, while holding secretly to the religion of his father. This usually is not evident until there is a death in the family, at which time the Christian, not wishing to offend or dishonor his ancestors, often reverts to his old Buddhist forms.

The only way this kind of bondage could be broken, the pastor said, was for the Christian to make an open declaration in which he said: "I renounce the gods of my father," or "I renounce the gods of my ancestors." Of course this is tantamount to saying "I hate father and mother," but it is necessary in order to throw off the yoke and enter into wholeness.

Several years ago my wife made friends with a beautiful young woman whose father had been an American diplomat in India. Although he had been a member of an institutional church, he felt he should not offend his Indian friends by flaunting his religion. Instead, he embraced many of the outward accoutrements of the Hindu faith, filling his house with statues, idols, and various Hindu trappings.

When he left India, he brought these idols, many of them made of gold, jade, and carved teak, back to the States. After his death, his daughter inherited them and placed them in her beautiful home in the Pocono Mountains of Pennsylvania.

We became acquainted with her when she attended a luncheon where I spoke. Across the next few months we corresponded and the following summer we paid a brief visit to her lovely home. Shortly after she had become a Christian, her husband had left her, which only intensified her desire for inner healing. As Jackie helped her, it became evident that some obstacle held her to the past. She could not break clear of her father's powerful influence over her life.

As they prayed together, the woman realized her father's influence was in some way connected to the various idols and statues which filled the house. Before the day was over, the two of them had an idol breaking/burning ceremony. Those which were made of flammable material were burned in the fireplace. The others were broken and smashed outside on the patio and dumped into the lake. Many of the statues and figures were worth hundreds, maybe thousands, of dollars. But the price was a small one to pay for the tremendous release that came from it.

Sometimes it is easier to deal with a living problem than a dead memory. A young widow moved to Melbourne from West Palm Beach where she had lived prior to her husband's death. Because he did not have adequate insurance, she was left virtually penniless. The only thing she salvaged from the estate was their large, expensive house in West Palm Beach which her husband, a contractor, had built shortly before he died. It was filled with a short lifetime of memories, but since she had been promised a job in Melbourne, she had moved her children up the coast to go to work.

When we learned of her, she had lost her job and was living on food stamps, trying to keep the three small children warm around a tiny wood stove in a cheap duplex apartment.

Some of our men visited with her, and after finding out her circumstances, counseled her to sell the big house in West Palm Beach which, because of its location, had remained empty even though she had tried repeatedly to rent it. They showed her how she could realize enough money from the sale, not only to purchase a nice house in Melbourne, but to put the balance in savings so she could live off the interest.

"You don't understand," she wept, "I can't sell that house. It's all I have left of my husband."

Fortunately they were able to show her the need for healing in this area. She saw it and accepted their help. The house brought in more money than any of them had anticipated.

The renunciation of the idols of tradition and the tyranny of ancestors will always result in a time of trial. In the life of Hezekiah, from the moment he was crowned king until he finally died, he was always being tempted to return to the way of his father. Even though he had been healed inwardly and set free from tyranny, many of those around him were unwilling to accept this new way of life. Thus the conflict and tension remained.

When King Sennacherib learned that Hezekiah was not going to follow the course of his father, the Assyrian king gathered his troops and marched on Jerusalem. They surrounded the walled city—185,000 of them—and began to shout in Hebrew, "Return to the gods of Ahab, return to the gods of your father."

It was a tense moment. The people of Jerusalem, who wanted to be true to their new king, felt the pressure. All they had to do was renounce this new way of living and return to the worship of idols. If they did, the Assyrians would withdraw. If they continued loyal to Hezekiah and his God, the Assyrians would overrun the city and kill them.

Throughout the night the Assyrians milled around the

walls of the city, crying out in Hebrew, "Return to the gods of Ahab."

Hezekiah sat in his chambers, listening, and perhaps at the same time hearing the murmuring of the people in the streets below.

"All you have to do is give allegiance to your daddy," the tempter was saying.

That's a low blow, any way you look at it. But that is the way Satan always fights, playing on the sentiments, trying to bring us back into bondage by quoting Scripture. "I know your father wasn't a godly man, but at least he kept the city from being overrun. The mothers were able to raise their children in peace and the men were free to support their families. Now, in the morning, the city is going to be sacked. The men will be carried off as slaves, the women raped, and you, the king, will be beheaded. The Bible says 'Honor thy father and mother that your days may be long upon the land.' Now, because you have broken that commandment, your days are about to be cut off. All you have to do is restore the honor due to your dear old father."

But Hezekiah had already made his decision. "I will not return to bondage," he said. "Nor will I lead the people back into idolatry."

He called for his old friend, the prophet Isaiah, who had received his call the same year Hezekiah's grandfather, King Uzziah, had died. "Come with me," Hezekiah said. "Let's stand on the walls and trust God to deliver us."

Sometime during the night a host of angels appeared among the Assyrians. Frightened and confused, the Assyrians began fighting with each other, and when the people arose the next morning to face what they felt was certain death, they found the entire Assyrian army had been slaughtered. King Sennacherib, seeing the slaughter, turned in fear and ran all the way back to Nineveh where his own sons killed him.

The final victory always belongs to God, but He seldom delivers His servants from their bondages in the flick of an eye. More often our initial commitments to Him, like Hezekiah's decision to turn from Ahab's god to the Lord, are tested, and thereby deepened, unto our lives' ends. Every day we must choose anew to follow Jesus.

10

CONTENTMENT . . . NOW

We had just finished our evening meal and the family was sitting comfortably around the table, enjoying small talk and catching up on the day's activities. Summer was drawing to a close and in a few days the children would be back in school. Our oldest son, Bruce, had already left for college in Oklahoma, leaving behind a sadly vacant chair at the table. Tim, who had just come in from football practice, had eaten everything on his plate and was now systematically attacking and finishing every other bowl of food on the table. The two older teenage girls, Robin, who was a freshman at the local community college, and Bonnie, who was a senior in high school, were laughing at Tim as he devoured the last scraps of food. Trim and beautiful, they were very careful about what they ate and what they wore. If their younger brother wanted to act like a human garbage disposal, that was all right, but not for them. Our youngest daughter, Sandy, who at twelve thought she was twenty, but still acted like a fifth-grader, was eager for me to "dismiss the troops'' so she could get back out in the yard and play with her friends. After all, there were only four days left in the summer vacation and then it was back to school. She needed to make use of every available second to play.

Suddenly there was a heavy knocking at the door. Sandy, looking for some excuse to leave the table anyway, shouted, "I'll get it!" But before she could get her chair pushed back from the table the front door burst open, framing the lanky figure of one of the young men in the church fellowship. His face was flushed from the wind, having just gotten off his motorcycle. Removing his helmet, he stepped into the dining room and asked excitedly, "Is it true? I mean about next Saturday?"

"You'll have to do better than that," I shrugged, motioning him into the room. "What about next Saturday?"

"You mean you haven't heard? Everybody I know is talking about it."

The kids were all ears. Even Tim had stopped eating and was listening intently. Our caller looked around the room and finally realized we were ignorant of his great news. He shook his head.

"Well, I was on the phone with an old friend up in West Virginia last night. He told me that everybody up there was really upset. The world is supposed to come to an end on September 6. That's Saturday."

Tim resumed his eating. "So, what's the rush," he said. "Today's only Wednesday."

It was the kind of answer I would have expected my children to give, the kind I would have hoped they would give. Sandy looked at me plaintively and said, "Daddy, can I go outside now? I've got only an hour before I have to come back in and all the kids are out there waiting for me."

I nodded my head and she was out the door. What was the end of the world when the neighborhood gang wanted to ride skateboards in our driveway? I looked up at the young man and motioned for him to sit down in Sandy's empty chair. "Have a piece of pie, Tony, and tell me all about it."

There wasn't much to tell. A lot of people were excited about a rumor that the world was coming to an end. It seemed some religious sect was going door-to-door across the nation—in fact, we later learned it was across the world—warning people to get ready. September 6, 1975, was The End.

Of course it wasn't. Since it was the last Saturday before school, we crammed it full of all kinds of kid activities. I took Tim and Sandy water skiing, while Robin and Bonnie spent the day at the beach, trying to soak in the last drop of sunshine before they returned to the classrooms. Jackie went to the beauty shop and then spent the afternoon in the quiet house alone, catching up on everything that needed to be done before school started. In short, we did all the normal Saturday things. Of course, there was the possibility the prophecy might be right, but it would have been right only by accident. Our kids knew this, and it really didn't make much difference to them. To be with the Lord was their final destination anyway, in the meantime they intended to enjoy life here on earth.

We hear a lot of reports these days about the end of the world. We shouldn't be surprised. The Bible says that as the end approaches there will be wild rumors of all sorts, reporting Christ has returned in one place or another. However, Jesus said that not even the Son of God knew when the end would come. That information belonged to the Father alone. Jesus did have a word to say to us about the last days:

> *These things I have spoken unto you that in me ye might have peace. In the world ye shall have tribulation: but be of good cheer; I have overcome the world (John 16:33).*

History is fraught with tales of groups of people who sold all their belongings and fled to the mountaintops or hid themselves away in caves to await the end of the world. It seems that the unhealed man is always setting dates, hoping for the worst. Like the Broadway singer, he cries out: "Stop the world, I want to get off." Why? Because he has not experienced the contentment of life which is possible on this earth, and thus yearns for anything that will get him out of here.

Inner healing, however, produces a different type of person. As a person moves into transparency of soul, into maturity of the Spirit, as the inner lake is cleansed and the old wounds and hurts healed (and even our thoughts brought into captivity to the obedience of Jesus Christ), the discontentment fades away and life with God here on earth grows more meaningful. To the person who has experienced inner healing, the world itself grows more beautiful, friends are friendlier, loved ones more precious, life more abundant, and he sees the face of God in every dewdrop and hears His voice in every murmur of the breeze.

The great purpose of the Holy Spirit is to show us how to live every day to its fullest, to usher us into the kingdom of God right here on earth. There is no need to wait until we die to experience the joy, bliss, and security of heaven; no need to project our misery and insecurity on the world by setting false dates and making preposterous claims concerning the "rapture." There may be a rapture. There will certainly be tribulation. But that is all inconsequential when you are living in the joy of the Lord one day at a time.

Yet it is at this place that most of us have our greatest difficulty. An old friend of mine once told of taking a train trip down the eastern seaboard. At noon he made his way from his compartment back to the dining car where the steward seated him with a middle-aged couple who had already ordered their food. The husband seemed friendly enough, but his wife complained about everything. She complained about the silver on the table, she found a speck of dust in her water and demanded the waiter send it back, she grumbled about the bumpy ride, the food, and the service.

In an effort to try to lighten what was an extremely heavy situation, my friend asked the man what he did for a living.

"I'm a banker," the man said, "but my wife is in the manufacturing business."

"Oh, what does she manufacture?"

My friend said the man had the most sorrowful look he had ever seen when he said softly, so his wife (who was complaining to the waiter about the lettuce) couldn't hear. "Unhappiness," the man said sadly. "Every place she goes she manufactures unhappiness."

We all know people like that. Maybe we are one ourselves. It is the result of an unhealed spirit, the result of trying to cope with today's tribulation without the good cheer that comes by being filled with the Spirit of Christ.

At a dinner party recently I sat across the table from a distinguished attorney. When he discovered I was a minister he said, "Oh, what a wonderful occupation. Some day you are going to grow old, and when you do you will look back with great satisfaction on the work you have done. I realize things are probably tough now, but when you get to be my age and look back, it will all seem worthwhile."

I had to stop him. "Friend, I hate to disillusion you, but I'm satisfied right now. I don't have to wait until I grow older and look back to find my joy. I'm living in so much contentment now I can hardly stand it."

He said he understood, but I could tell from the expression on his face that he didn't. He was a typical mask-wearer, yet I knew behind his gracious smile and pleasing manner lay buried the anguish of a lifetime.

Jesus sent the Holy Spirit into the world to give us con-

177

tentment now. That's difficult for some to understand. They cling to the Gospel as a life preserver to keep them afloat in a sea of despair. In one sense of the word, that's true. But the Gospel is far more than a life preserver. The Gospel is actually the good news that even though we have tribulation in this world, we have something to shout about: Jesus has overcome the world. He sent His Holy Spirit to bring us into the same fulfillment, the same inner health that He had when He was here on earth. Contentment, joy, wholeness—not later on, but now.

Tragically, many Christians miss out on all that because they reject the Holy Spirit. Seeing only the more sensational "gift ministries"—the prophets, the healers, the miracle workers—they fail to understand that the real purpose of the coming of the Spirit is to lead us into abundant living through Jesus Christ.

It's strange, but the very things God has designed to bring us pleasure are often the things that cause us the most frustration. Why? Because in most cases we treat these things as a means to an end, rather than seeing them as a joyful end in themselves.

One of my favorite ministers is James Lee Beall, pastor of the Bethesda Missionary Temple in Detroit. In one of his little teaching booklets, Jim Beall pointed this out. He said, "We read for profit, we party for contacts, we lunch for contracts, we bowl for unity, we drive for mileage, we gamble for charity, we go out in the evening for the greater joys of the municipality, we stay at home on the weekend to rebuild our home—always looking for some other reason for doing things." What a rat race we have gotten ourselves into.

The Christian faith is extremely functional. The best example of how functional it is comes from the Book of Philippians. Here Paul, chained in a prison cell, locked in a dungeon with shackles around his arms and legs, writes back to the church at Philippi and says, "Wow, what a ball I'm having here, folks!'' He had learned that real contentment is not based on our circumstances, but springs from inner healing.

Listen to Paul in Philippians 4 as he sings from his prison cell:

Rejoice in the Lord alway: and again I say rejoice.
Let your moderation be known unto all men.
The Lord is at hand.
[There's no need to wait for the second coming, He is at hand now.]
Be careful for nothing; but in everything by prayer and supplication with thanksgiving let your requests be made known unto God. And the peace of God, which passeth all understanding, shall keep your hearts and minds through Christ Jesus.
[Inner healing, in a nutshell, is achieved when your heart and mind is ''kept'' by the peace which God gives through Christ Jesus.]
Finally, brethren, whatsoever things are true,
whatsoever things are honest,
whatsoever things are just,
whatsoever things are pure,
whatsoever things are lovely,
whatsoever things are of good report;
if there be any virtue, if there be any praise,
think on these things.

For several years I have been aware of the importance of going to sleep thinking on ''these things''—the things that are honest, just, pure, lovely, and of good report. And if it is important for my inner health, how much more important it is for my young children whose minds are still a fertile garden into which I have the opportunity of sowing weeds or productive fruit, tares or wheat. For the last several years, when I am home

179

at night, I have made the rounds of the children in their beds, kneeling down beside them or sitting quietly on the edge of the bed, talking about things of virtue and praise. It may have been a bad day for them. Tim may have been chewed out by his coach at ball practice, but he needs to hear from me, his daddy, that I am proud of him. He needs to hear me recount some of the joys of the day and how good it is to have a son who is growing into manhood. I want him to go to sleep on that thought, for I know that during his sleeping hours the Holy Spirit will be much at work in his subconscious, bringing him to total inner healing.

In the case of Robin and Bonnie, their needs are different. Approaching the time when they will leave home, they are faced with the problems and frustrations of decisions. They may need to talk for a few minutes and allow me to respond, dropping into the garden of their hearts seeds that will grow and produce lovely flowers which will bloom in sweet fragrance. I want them to know how much I love them, how proud I am of them despite any defects they may have experienced during the day.

It was because of this inner health that our seventeen-year-old Robin was able to go through a very trying experience last year. Driving our little Vega down a main street near the high school, she went through a stoplight and crashed into the side of another car. She was clearly to blame. The car was almost demolished and it was only by the grace of God that the boy in the other car was not killed. Most of the day was spent getting X-rays at the hospital, filling out police, insurance, and hospital forms. She was told she would have to appear in court, and of course our insurance company would have to pay all the bills.

That night I slipped into her darkened bedroom, expecting to find her unnerved, fearful, and crying. Instead she heard me coming and I heard her soft, cheerful, "Hi, dad." I sat down on the edge of her bed and took her hand.

"You okay, sweetheart?"

"I'm fine, dad," she said. "My knee hurts where I bumped it, but it's okay."

"The angel of the Lord was with you," I said softly.

"I know," she answered and squeezed my hand. "But he is always, isn't he?"

I nodded in the darkness, lay my hand on her head, and prayed for God's peace to keep her mind and heart during the night.

"Thanks, dad," she whispered and leaned up and kissed me. Then with a simple "Good night," she turned over and went to sleep.

He giveth his beloved sleep (Psalm 127:2).

That's the evidence of a mind that has spent its waking hours thinking on "these things."

Every child's needs are different. My "daddy responsibility," as the keeper of the garden of their hearts, is to make sure the right seeds are planted, the bushes trimmed, and the fruit harvested at the correct time. For instance, our twelve-year-old Sandy went through her growth period early. Last year she sprouted almost five inches and suddenly she was almost a foot taller than all her other friends, who would probably sprout up the next year. It was a grave cause of concern in her mind. Often when I would tuck her in and spend those few private moments which she knew were "just hers," she would tell me about her fear that she was going to be a giant.

"What if I never stop growing?" she asked. "What if I just keep on getting taller and taller? I don't want to be a freak."

It was a critical issue with her, and the wrong thoughts could warp and twist her mind for years to come. So many young girls go through this same thing, but because they allow thoughts of fear rather than thoughts of cheer inside their minds, they try to cover their rapid growth by stooping. Stooping eventually becomes a lifestyle, evidencing itself not only in a bent back and drooping shoulders, but by stooping in areas of self-confidence. Many a girl has gone through life bent over, telling herself and others around her that she's just a "freak," when actually she is a princess in the kingdom of God.

Thus it was often necessary for me to spend extra moments with Sandy, telling her how proud I was of her and sharing with her little stories of people who grew fast and grew slow, but all finally grew to be just the height God intended.

What a person thinks is extremely important. Especially is it important to control our last conscious thoughts before we go to sleep, thinking only on those things of "good report." It is often in the sleeping hours that the Holy Spirit is most active in His work of inner healing.

The great book on inner healing is the book of Proverbs. Its thirty-one chapters lend themselves ideally to daily reading, one chapter a day for the month, which means one could read the entire book twelve times a year, or over a ten-year period (which I recommend), it would be read one hundred twenty times.

It was the writer of Proverbs who said:

> *For as a man thinketh in his heart, so is he (Proverbs 23:7).*

Positive thinking and positive living are necessary if we expect to enter into inner healing. This is also true if we expect others around us to have inner healing, for our negative thoughts can be just as damaging to them as if we had opened their minds and poured in poison.

Last month our daughter Bonnie, a senior in high school, came home bubbling with excitement. She had received an invitation from a friend to spend the spring holidays in the mountains. There was only one catch. They would have to drive one of our cars.

Ordinarily this would have presented no problem and I would have shared her joy and excitement. That morning, however, after Bonnie had left for school, I had discovered oil leaking out from under the station wagon. I carefully drove it to the garage and was told we had serious engine problems. Thus when Bonnie came bouncing in and broke her good news, I reacted, and tossed her a negative thought in exchange. Before I realized it, I had destroyed all her happy plans, outlining reason after reason why such a trip was out of the question. Moments before she had been "all joy," now she was filled with despair. She finally muttered, "Oh, let's forget it," and walked out of the room.

I stood there for a long time, thinking. Was it possible that I had wounded her with my negative spirit? That's not to say I should not say no. But I should have at least listened to her story, and then told her our circumstances. I should have allowed her the dignity of reaching the right conclusion without it being forced on her from the outside. Instead I tried to control her.

In Paul's letter to the Philippians he talks about his own positive example which he hoped would bring inner healing to his friend in Philippi.

Those things, which ye have both learned and received and heard and seen in me, do: and the God of peace shall be with you (Philippians 4:9).

Then he injects something else which we often miss. The Roman prison system felt no obligation to feed the prisoners. All they did was lock them up. If a prisoner starved, that was his bad fortune. Therefore, the only way a prisoner could stay alive was to hope someone on the outside would care enough to send food, or money to buy food. Paul was in this situation. In this case, he was looking to the church at Philippi for his support. He was at the financial mercy of his friends. He writes them saying:

> *But I rejoiced in the Lord greatly, that now at the last your care of me hath flourished again; wherein ye were also careful, but ye lacked opportunity (Philippians 4:10).*

It's hard to believe, but it seems that for a time his friends had actually forgotten about him. A man can get very hungry in a situation like that. Now, though, they had begun to help him again and Paul was writing to thank them, and to let them know that he understood the reason they had neglected him in the past was they "lacked opportunity."

From his letter, and his attitude, we begin to understand something of the open, loving, transparent nature of this man Paul. Yet, if ever a man had reason to live a life of reaction, it was Paul. He had been stoned, rejected, cursed, and was now in prison for something he didn't do. He was having to depend on friends who often forgot about him—yet he responded only in love.

> *Not that I speak in respect of want: for I have learned, in whatsoever state I am, therewith to be content. I know both how to be abased, and I know how to abound: everywhere and in all things I am instructed both to be full and to be hungry, both to abound and to suffer need. I can do all things through Christ which strengtheneth me (Philippians 4:11-13).*

While he appreciated the material gifts and possessions he had, Paul made it very clear that he was not dependent on these things for happiness. Contentment, he said, goes far beyond financial security, good health, a job, or respect in the community. There is no way to equate external prosperity with happiness and contentment. These things spring only from a mind that has been transformed by the renewing presence of the Holy Spirit.

Jim Beall once talked about a man who has everything. His clothes are given to him, he has three good meals a day furnished without charge, and a private room of his own. He is protected from those who would try to harm him by armed guards. He has no rent to pay and no major decisions to make. He has maximum security with a guaranteed future of minimum risk. But no man in his right mind would want to trade places with him because he is serving a life sentence in the state penitentiary. He has all the external trappings of security, but he is the perfect illustration that contentment is not found in outer circumstances. It has to come from within, from the renewed mind that brings us into a state of happiness and contentment designed for every situation.

I found myself observing one of those situations in the summer of 1975. I took off a few days so I could accompany my parents on a trip they needed to make from their summer home near Asheville, North Carolina, to Rochester, Minnesota, where they were both to undergo medical check ups at Mayo Clinic. At eighty-five, daddy could not walk without two canes and could not climb stairs at all. Mother was in her late seventies and could navigate a bit better. Both of them, however, indicated they would feel better if I flew with them to Rochester. Since I was supposed to be in Minneapolis the next day, I found it easy to arrange my schedule.

Traveling was difficult for daddy in particular. The muscles in his legs had atrophied, making it necessary for him to use a wheelchair if he had to walk more than just a few steps. This was their first airplane trip in more than a year, and he was apprehensive about getting on and off the plane, the use of a wheelchair when they changed planes in Chicago, and a dozen other matters. I knew my presence would ease their anxiety.

Both mother and daddy are very orderly persons. Daddy's workshop behind the house is as well appointed and organized as a surgical clinic. Every tool has its special place. All the nails have been sorted according to size and shape and put in separate glass jars. The same is true with nuts, bolts, washers, and screws. Cans of paint are labeled and sealed. Bits of string and wire are carefully wrapped and kept separate. The floor is spotlessly clean.

Inside the house things are the same. Mother's pantry is better organized than the grocery store. Clothes in the closet are on hangers all spaced two fingers apart. Things in the drawers are neatly folded. There is no dirt under the carpet and no dust on the top of the window sills. They live a very ordered, regulated life, rising at the same hour each morning and going to bed at the same hour each night. They have lived this way for years, and even today I know if I visit their house I will find the whisk broom hung on the same nail in the same closet where it was hung thirty years ago.

Even though this kind of regularity is commendable, it gave me an uneasy feeling when I thought of the trip to Rochester. They had planned it for weeks, packing and repacking their bags. Mother insisted they take along their breakfast bran and canned prune juice which had been their breakfast diet (often supplemented with fresh fruit) for the last twenty years. She also packed their pillows. "Those pillows in the hotel and clinic just aren't comfortable," she said. She would have taken their bedboards, but the manager at the hotel in Rochester had assured her they would be provided.

Friends drove us to the airport at Asheville. I checked their bags and arranged for the special chair so the attendants could carry Daddy up the steps of the plane. The only luggage they carried with them was a large shopping bag with some books, grapes, raisins, saltine crackers, and mother's knitting. We were scheduled to change planes in Chicago in order to arrive in Rochester by 5:00 p.m. This would give them plenty of time to check into the hotel and get ready for their appointment at the clinic two days later.

Then the very worst thing that could possibly happen, happened. Like Job, "that which I feared came upon me." We arrived at Chicago's O'Hare Airport, the busiest airport in the world, only to discover Northwest Orient Airlines had gone on strike. There was no possible way to get to Rochester that night.

With mother and daddy in wheelchairs, we were caught in an angry mass of shoving, shouting people in front of the Northwest counter.

"No planes, no planes," the agent was shouting. "Come back tomorrow morning and we'll get you on a commuter flight."

I looked at my folks, virtually helpless. I finally got to the agent and asked if there was any way we could claim their bags, since it looked like we would have to spend the night in Chicago. He shook his head in a futile gesture. "This place is a madhouse. The baggage handlers are threatening to go on strike themselves. There's no way to get their bags. Just pick them up in Rochester after you arrive."

A limousine took us to a nearby motel. We had to take special pains helping daddy in and out of the car and then helping him as he leaned heavily on his canes down the long corridor to their room.

Having traveled extensively, I knew always to carry the necessities with me. Thus I had my toilet kit in my brief case, along with a change of socks and underwear. But for my parents, it was an entirely different matter. They had nothing with them except a few grapes, raisins, and their Bibles. No night clothes. No toothbrushes. Nothing. Besides this, the beds in their motel room looked like they had been used by elephants.

They were lumpy and sway-backed with the flattest pillows I had ever seen.

"Oh, Lord," I prayed, "what are they going to do?"

I learned something that evening. All those years my parents had walked with the Lord had brought about an inner healing I never dreamed existed. When the chips were down, they revealed their real natures—and it so resembled Jesus it took my breath. Yes, mother and daddy had grown comfortable in their daily routine. They liked everything in its place and fussed a little when things weren't proper. But when all those things were taken away, I discovered they were just as much at home with nothing as they were with everything. In fact, they were far more yielding than I was. When I expressed my deep concern over their having to spend the night without any of their regular comforts—even pajamas—it was my eighty-five-year-old father who paraphrased Paul's motto back to me:

> *For I have learned, in whatsoever state I am, even without a cup to put my false teeth in, therewith to be content.*

The Gospel of Jesus Christ is the most functional philosophy in the world.

Back in the fall of last year I saw how that same principle had been worked into another family. Jackie and I attended a wedding rehearsal party for a young couple in our church. At our table was a retired CPA who had recently moved to Florida from Pennsylvania. We chatted amiably and I found him and his wife to be charming, sensitive people. During the conversation, they mentioned their son, who they said was retarded. Half of each year was spent in an institutional school, the rest of the time he lived with them.

"How old is he?" I asked.

"He's forty-three," the father answered. Then he added, "He's our only son and the doctors say he will never change. Sometimes he's dangerous to himself and others, but we have found that through love he can be controlled."

"Forty-three," I thought. "That's my age. And he's been that way all his life."

The woman, soft-spoken, gray-haired, with an air of great tenderness about her, spoke. "He's a very loving boy. Very gentle. It's only when he's frustrated that he acts violently."

"You've kept him at home for forty-three years?" I asked.

"Yes, only he is in the institution half of the year."

"Then you have actually patterned and programmed your entire lives around his need, haven't you?" I asked.

I saw the man, dignified, yet very warm, reach over and take his wife's hand. "Very few people understand," he said. "But he is our son, and nothing is more important than loving him into happiness and healing. We believe that somehow, through our love, God will bring him into wholeness."

We sat for a long time, not speaking. I could feel the moisture gathering in my eyes and suddenly was afraid I would embarrass them by crying. I changed the subject and we chatted on about something else, but I felt like I had been treading on holy soil. Deep within me was a desire to take off my shoes.

"God must be something like that," I said to Jackie as we left to drive home.

"No, they are something like God," she corrected.

Whatever the case, I knew I had been in the presence of people who had learned the secret of contentment. They could say with Paul, "In whatsoever state I am—even if it means I have a retarded son who is forty-three years old who will live with us until he is seventy—therewith to be content. Because I can do all things through Christ which strengtheneth me."

God doesn't promise us a rose garden. He promises us

tribulation. But in the midst of that—perhaps even because of it—we can be of good cheer because He has overcome the world.

This is what "risky living" is all about. A person can seek the kingdoms of this world or the kingdom of God. If he chooses this world he will go after things: houses, real estate, position, reputation, popularity, sensual gratification—all the things the world calls security. Or, he can seek the kingdom of God, risking everything on Jesus' promise to bring us into happiness and maturity.

To move into this realm of maturity calls for a total death to self. It means you are willing to be expendable, to give up all self-rights for the happiness of others. It means you submit yourself to the loving hand of God much as a pawn submits to a chessmaster: "In whatsoever square you choose to place me, there will I be content." So even if you are surrounded by knights, rooks, and bishops who desire to destroy you, you will raise your hands in praise and say, "Hallelujah! I'm expenda-ble. I choose to give up my life for the glory of the King."

Risky living. But in dying we find life.

When I was a boy, people used to talk about the "poorhouse." I never knew what the poorhouse was, I had never seen one, nor had I talked with anyone who had seen one. Everybody knew, though, that it was a terrible place on the back side of a lonely hill where a family went when they ran out of money.

As a result of this horrible fear of the poorhouse, I grew up hoarding my money. Every dime I earned was stashed away and we spent money only for bare necessities. I still have some of that tendency left, for we have continued, across the years, to live frugally. However, when we were exposed to some of these kingdom principles—especially the one that states that in order to receive you must give—it presented an acute crisis in my spirit. If I gave, even if I gave away only the tithe which is the basic minimum, I was running the risk of winding up in the poorhouse.

I was encouraged by the story of William Carey, a young English shoe cobbler of the late eighteenth century. Carey believed God wanted him to carry the Gospel to the people of India. The leaders of his church in England ridiculed him. Finally, with stern, theological authority they told him if God wanted the people of India saved, He'd do it sovereignly—without the help of a shoe cobbler. Carey, however, was a man fashioned in the likeness of the Apostles. He left England and sailed to India to become the first modern day Protestant missionary—daring to do that which others called impossible. Even after all these years, Carey's motto still excites men who dare step out in faith:

Attempt great things for God;
Expect great things from God.

The Christian takes his direction from a different King. He is not motivated by money, fear, or public opinion. Nor does he shrink just because his way is blocked by a mountain. He is like Thoreau's marcher, who hearing the sound of a different drummer, "steps to the music which he hears, however measured or far away."

The worst of all heresies is to despair of those childhood ideals, those dreams that stimulated us when our minds were still young. How many of us have reached the crisis of middle life and, disillusioned, put aside our resolves of faith because of the fantasies of fear?

"Too impossible," we say sadly. "Too foolish. Too risky."

No wonder Whittier wrote:

Of all sad words of tongue or pen,
The saddest are these, "It might have been."

In our home we are challenging our children to invest their futures in something that will cost them their lives—for the glory of God. We are challenging them to go out and, even at an early age, run the risk of dying for Jesus. Why settle for the poorhouse when you can go all the way and die on the cross.

The world does not understand this. The world says parents should protect their children from pain, hardship, and death—not point them toward it. But we know there is no joy anywhere outside that which is done strictly for the glory of God. Abundant life comes only when we give our lives totally and completely to that which God has called us to do.

The most exciting and whole people I know are those who leave the comforts and security of home, who turn their backs on well-paying jobs and worldly fame to go to the remote areas of the earth as missionary doctors, pilots, translators, and teachers. Many of them die on foreign soil, unrecognized by men. But the price of death is very small when compared to what they purchase by their risky living. After all, what's the use of living if you don't attempt the impossible.

Risky living puts you in the position where God will eventually take off your mask, peel back all your layers, and lay you bare for the world to see. However, if the process of inner healing has been thorough and complete, those who look into your life from the outside will not see your nakedness, but instead—through your transparency—will see the glory of the One in whose image you have been created.